WHAT YOUR COLLEAGUES ARE SAYING . . .

As educators, we are challenged in preparing our students for college and career readiness as they go into the real world. Developing Expert Learners addresses the intentional moves of the teacher to prepare students for challenging work at their level of learning, resulting in students reaching their fullest potential as experts in their own learning.

—**Elizabeth Alvarez**, Chief of Schools
Chicago Public Schools
Chicago, IL

"Teaching for transfer"—imparting knowledge and skill in a way that makes them really useful, and not just fodder for exams and tests—is the Holy Grail of education. This book is a wonderfully practical guide to how to do it in any classroom.

—**Guy Claxton**, Author
The Learning Power Approach: Teaching Learners to Teach Themselves

This book is the roadmap to take students from being developing experts to the experts they all have the potential to be. Providing high expectations and valuing all students as learners requires educators to plan instruction that takes students—all students—from their current level, to that place just beyond that level. McDowell suggests that in order for students to become experts, "the control over learning must be mutually shared between teachers and students." Teaching students how to build their efficacy in learning, the ability to navigate and lead their own learning, is the optimal approach for every faculty to engage in. McDowell identifies The 5Cs (Clarify, Challenge, Check, Communicate, and Cross contexts) that are requisite for this shared partnership to flourish, and gives reflection questions and activities that allow every educator to plan their steps toward this desirable result.

—**Tom Hierck**
Consultant/Author
Grading for Impact: Raising Student Achievement
Through a Target-Based Assessment and Learning System

D1451869

As he did in Rigorous PBL by Design, *Michael McDowell has once again produced an invaluable resource for educators who are striving to empower students to fully develop their own expertise and self-efficacy.* Developing Expert Learners *provides the practical means—through planning tools, research-based strategies, teaching practices, and special features—to enable teachers to maximize student learning at the surface, deep, and transfer levels of complexity. By integrating "The 5Cs (Clarify, Challenge, Check, Communicate, and Cross Contexts) as guiding actions for developing student expertise" into all unit and lesson planning, McDowell shows how these strategies can dramatically impact student learning. Classroom educators will find Chapter 3, "Planning for Impact," and Chapter 4, "Teaching for Impact" particularly useful for creating and implementing their own roadmap to greater student self-efficacy. Chapter 5, "Collective Efficacy," presents a powerful framework that teacher teams can utilize to create their own beliefs and action steps to greater student learning.*

—Larry Ainsworth, Author
Common Formative Assessments 2.0, and *Learning Intentions and Success Criteria*

I appreciate and am enthusiastic about the layout of this book. For a coach, team leader, or school administrator, the book lends itself to being a manual for school improvement. It provides excellent questions to reflect on and activities after each chapter for school leaders to collaborate with and work alongside teacher teams in developing efficacy and expertise at their schools—which in the end will impact the achievement of all our learners. Our district will benefit from the content of this book and its resources, activities, and reflection questions to increase student learning at the surface, deep, and transfer levels through the work of teams.

—LeeAnn Lawlor
Assistant Superintendent of Educational Services
Cartwright Elementary School District

This urgently needed book has the potential to transform schools and experiences for learners and teachers everywhere. Once again, Michael McDowell has written a compelling, practical guide for educators who seek to give their students the skills they need to be successful in our ever-changing world. This book is a must-read for new and veteran educators alike!

—Cindy Johanson
Executive Director, Edutopia
George Lucas Educational Foundation

Of course, Michael McDowell has once again provided a purposeful and practical guide for teachers and leaders. Teachers, administrators, and even student leaders recognize the importance of focusing on learning through clear learning intentions, success criteria, and now—with this new book—tools and strategies to measure student progress. We have made a fundamental shift in how we address instructional practice, review student work, and more important, build our own efficacy and expertise at all levels of our organization.

—Maren Rocca Hunt
Executive Director, Elementary Education
Napa Valley Unified School District

In Developing Expert Learners, *McDowell harnesses the research on building student self-efficacy, peer-to-peer feedback structures, and student ownership of learning through a handful of focus areas, aligned and actionable learning practices, and tools that have been road-tested. If you wish to build stronger, more invested, and more equipped learners, this book is a must-read.*

—Kara Vandas
Consultant, Co-Author of *Clarity for Learning*

As a follow up to Rigorous PBL by Design, *McDowell continues to write about practical strategies to help teachers build students' expertise. The book is filled with strategies, tools, and very useful references based on the exciting research of John Hattie and* Visible Learning. *McDowell shapes this book around 5Cs—promoting clarity, leveraging challenge, consistent checking, cultivating conversation, and tackling contextually rich problems. Michael's command of lesson design and instruction make this a natural follow up to his very successful* Rigorous PBL by Design. *It will clearly help teachers have impact on student learning.*

—Ainsley B. Rose
Corwin Author Consultant

As we move away from the age of pouring knowledge into the brains of learners and, instead, begin handing them the steering wheel of their own learning to develop efficacy and expertise, McDowell's tool kit of sound simplicity, sparked by wisdom and courage, offers clear and do-able courses of action that all educators can put into motion to change the learning lives of their students.

—Melissa Schaub
Director of Learning
The Anglo-American School of Moscow

Developing Expert Learners *is a practitioner guide for the research-based classroom teacher. McDowell does an exemplary job of providing powerful strategies that can transform any classroom into a learning laboratory. The book is filled with these strategies, relevant school-based examples, and educator testimonials that inspire. McDowell focuses on the importance of both the learner and the teacher in helping to co-construct a learning community that empowers learners to attain high levels of expertise and efficacy. The book is a wonderful balance between theory and practice and a must have for any educator trying to move their students from surface to deep understanding. McDowell brings action to research.*

—Sascha Heckmann
Head of American International School of Mozambique
Author of *Personalized Learning in a PLC at Work*

Michael McDowell provides practical examples in designing learning for students. Developing Expert Learners *is a must-read for educators to build student expertise in a meaningful way, with many wonderful thoughts and ideas to support teachers in developing clarity for their students.*

—Sophie Murphy
Melbourne Graduate School of Education
University of Melbourne

Developing Expert Learners

Developing Expert Learners

A Roadmap for Growing Confident and Competent Students

Michael McDowell

Foreword by James Nottingham / Afterword by Shirley Clarke

FOR INFORMATION:

Corwin
A SAGE Company
2455 Teller Road
Thousand Oaks, California 91320
(800) 233-9936
www.corwin.com

SAGE Publications Ltd.
1 Oliver's Yard
55 City Road
London EC1Y 1SP
United Kingdom

SAGE Publications India Pvt. Ltd.
B 1/I 1 Mohan Cooperative Industrial Area
Mathura Road, New Delhi 110 044
India

SAGE Publications Asia-Pacific Pte. Ltd.
18 Cross Street #10-10/11/12
China Square Central
Singapore 048423

Acquisitions Editor: Ariel Curry
Development Editor: Desirée A. Bartlett
Associate Content
    Development Editor: Jessica Vidal
Production Editor: Amy Schroller
Copy Editor: Karin Rathert
Typesetter: C&M Digitals (P) Ltd.
Proofreader: Dennis Webb
Indexer: Robie Grant
Cover Designer: Janet Kiesel
Marketing Manager: Margaret O'Connor

Copyright © 2019 by Corwin

All rights reserved. Except as permitted by U.S. copyright law, no part of this work may be reproduced or distributed in any form or by any means, or stored in a database or retrieval system, without permission in writing from the publisher.

When forms and sample documents appearing in this work are intended for reproduction, they will be marked as such. Reproduction of their use is authorized for educational use by educators, local school sites, and/or noncommercial or nonprofit entities that have purchased the book.

All third party trademarks referenced or depicted herein are included solely for the purpose of illustration and are the property of their respective owners. Reference to these trademarks in no way indicates any relationship with, or endorsement by, the trademark owner.

Printed in the United States of America

Library of Congress Cataloging-in-Publication Data

Names: McDowell, Michael (Michael P.), author.

Title: Developing expert learners : a roadmap for growing confident and competent students / Michael McDowell.

Description: Thousand Oaks, California : Corwin, a Sage Company, [2019] | Includes bibliographical references and index.

Identifiers: LCCN 2018052016 | ISBN 9781544337159 (pbk. : alk. paper)

Subjects: LCSH: Problem-based learning. | Inquiry-based learning. | Critical thinking—Study and teaching.

Classification: LCC LB1027.42 .M33 2019 | DDC 371.39—dc23
LC record available at https://lccn.loc.gov/2018052016

This book is printed on acid-free paper.

19 20 21 22 23 10 9 8 7 6 5 4 3 2 1

DISCLAIMER: This book may direct you to access third-party content via Web links, QR codes, or other scannable technologies, which are provided for your reference by the author(s). Corwin makes no guarantee that such third-party content will be available for your use and encourages you to review the terms and conditions of such third-party content. Corwin takes no responsibility and assumes no liability for your use of any third-party content, nor does Corwin approve, sponsor, endorse, verify, or certify such third-party content.

CONTENTS

Visit the companion website at
http://resources.corwin.com/DevelopingExpertLearners
for downloadable resources.

LIST OF ONLINE RESOURCES

To access these resources, visit the companion website at
http://resources.corwin.com/DevelopingExpertLearners

Video 2.1 Draft of Teddy's Work

Leveled Success Criteria Examples

Planning for Impact – Unit/Lesson/Examples

FOREWORD

I wish I had had this book when I was classroom teacher. My emphasis back then was to ensure my students were willing and able to step out of their comfort zone—that's what prompted me to create the Learning Pit. Yet, if I'd also had this latest book by Michael McDowell, then I could have helped my students contextualise and extend their learning far more effectively.

I wish I had had this book as a school leader. With it, I would have been in a much better position to develop collective efficacy across my teams. We could have also identified the most effective practices for deepening and extending student learning and then directed our energies accordingly.

So, I'm delighted to have read this book now, as the owner of a group of educational companies. The advice within it will help me lead my teams in supporting schools and districts even more effectively. We will start with the *5Cs Framework,* as this should help teaching staff and leaders develop a clearer system of planning and culture development. We will also be advocating that educators engage with Michael's proposal to develop efficacy as a collective effort between students and staff.

The framework for developing expertise and creating a culture of efficacy will, I think, be particularly popular amongst my team of teachers, leaders, and support staff. Furthermore, the fact that Michael has underpinned all of his proposals with the most compelling research will make the book even more appealing, I'm sure.

With all that said, I think the greatest gains for my team—and therefore for the educators we work with and, in turn, their students—will be in taking up the challenge to identify the *underdog* strategies. Beautifully illustrated in this book's introduction, underdog strategies are those that are rarely found within current habits or reverences and yet are very often the most efficacious. Examples can be found throughout this book, my favourite of which is the idea of "best fit." As Michael says, almost every strategy makes an impact on learning, but there are several strategies that have the highest probability of working at different levels of complexity (i.e., surface, deep, and transfer). So, the challenge for all of us in education is to find those strategies that work for the right student, at the right stage of their learning, and for the right purpose. This takes determination, open-mindedness, and professional reflection—and this book will show us all where to start.

So read on, dear colleague: Michael has given us more insight, more inspiration, and more guidance on how to improve learning for all. If that isn't worthy of our time, then I don't know what is!

—James Nottingham
Creator of The Learning Pit and
Director of Challenging Learning

ACKNOWLEDGMENTS

During my first year as a high school principal, I went to a conference and listened to world renowned presenters repeatedly cite John Hattie's *Visible Learning* research in their presentations. On the plane ride home from the conference, I read Professor Hattie's book and was immediately transformed as an educator. I sent Professor Hattie an email and said I wanted to learn everything I could to ensure that my staff and I were "seeing through the eyes of students" and that all "students viewed themselves as their own teachers." He directed me to a small elementary school in Auckland, New Zealand. I flew out to see the Stonefields School with my wife and three-year-old daughter and was completely taken aback by how Professor Hattie's research had been translated into actual practice. The level of expertise and efficacy the students demonstrated on that trip changed me as an educator and as a parent.

Since those experiences, I have led organizations, taught middle school and graduate courses, and led professional development around the world to infuse this work into classrooms and schools. The presentations and workshops I led were primarily based on what I learned from teachers and students in the classroom. As such, this book is dedicated to those educators and their continued work to improve student learning, their own practice, and the practice of their colleagues.

I would like to specifically recognize the amazing staff at Ross School who have truly transformed the learning lives of their learners. I would also like to thank Shirley Clarke and James Nottingham for their endorsement of this work. They are truly the frontrunners of this work, and I'm humbled to be a part of the process of making an impact on learning.

To my wife and children—thank you for your patience and support.

Publisher's Acknowledgments

Corwin gratefully acknowledges the contributions of the following reviewers:

Elizabeth Alvarez
Chief of Schools
Chicago Public Schools

Elizabeth Crane
Adjunct Professor, Instructional Leadership
Eastern Kentucky University

Clint Heitz
Instructional Coach
Bettendorf, IA

Elisa Waingort
Grade 4 Teacher
Calgary, AB, Canada

ABOUT THE AUTHOR

Michael McDowell, EdD, serves as the Superintendent of the Ross School District. During his tenure, the Ross School District has progressed to the top of California districts in relation to student connectedness and well-being as well as being in the top tier of districts in academic achievement and growth. Beyond academic achievement and social and emotional development, the Ross School District has emerged as a beacon for innovation, creating over 65+ different electives— from virtual game design and broadcast journalism—sponsoring the first TEDxYouth event in the Bay Area, and it is in the process of creating a service-learning and community engagement program for all students to serve the local and global community.

Prior to serving as a superintendent, Dr. McDowell served as an associate superintendent of instructional and personnel services and as a high school principal of a Title I and California Distinguished School. Before entering administration, he was a leadership and instructional coach, consulting with schools, districts, higher educational institutions, and state departments on educational leadership, teaching leadership, and instruction. Additionally, Dr. McDowell has several years of teaching experience in middle and high school science and mathematics.

Dr. McDowell serves as the Chair of the Advisory Board for One Percent of Education charged with facilitating leading experts in shaping a national narrative for advancing public education. Additionally, Dr. McDowell serves on the School of Environmental Leadership board tasked with scaling innovation in secondary school environments. Dr. McDowell also teaches graduate courses at San Francisco State University to aspiring educational leaders. Furthermore, Dr. McDowell is CEO of Hinge Education, LLC, supporting professional learning in educational systems around the world. He is an international presenter, speaking on instruction, learning, leadership, and innovation. He is an author and consultant with Corwin Press, providing services in problem and project-based learning, teaching and learning, systems and site leadership, and the Visible Learning Series. He is the author of *Rigorous PBL by Design: Three Key Shifts for Developing Confident and Competent Learners* (2017), *The Lead Learner: Increasing Clarity, Coherence and Capacity for All* (2018), and *Developing Student Expertise: A Guide for Ensuring Students Excel to High Levels of Achievement and Beyond* (2019).

Previously, Dr. McDowell was a national faculty member for the Buck Institute of Education, a school development coach at the New Tech Network, and an advisor to educational organizations focused on equity, excellence, and innovation. His practical expertise in schools and systems is complimented by his scholarly approach to leadership, learning, and instruction. He holds a BS, MA, and EdD. Michael and his wife Quinn live in Northern California with their two children Harper and Asher.

A TEACHER'S PERSPECTIVE

Early in my career, I experienced a professional learning event that fundamentally shifted my thinking and my practice. When I walked into the learning experience, projects, activities, and tasks were at the forefront of my mind. However, I walked out of the room understanding that student and teacher clarity about learning and growth must be at the forefront of all that we do in the classroom.

I was struck by the power clarity has in everything we do. The idea that students must focus on the learning expectations in the classroom (as opposed to the tasks they do), that they understand where they currently are in meeting those learning expectations, and that they know what next steps they need to take in their learning emerged as one of the greatest levers for impacting student learning and building student efficacy. To center my work, I began focusing my instructional design and my teaching practice on the following key questions for students:

Where am I going in my learning?

Where am I now in my learning?

What next steps am I going to take in my learning?

I realized that this type of questioning would be beneficial to use within my own classroom as I mentored learners and supported them in building their capacity to take ownership over their learning. I was extremely excited to implement these questions immediately with one particular 12th-grade student. I began by asking her to track her assessment progress over the school year.

After my professional learning experience, I realized that this assessment-tracking strategy had much more potential than simply tracking performance on *tasks* over time. I changed the focus of the assessment to the three questions and asked the student to articulate to me how her *learning* during each task was improving rather than how well she was completing each task. This shift in focus moved her away from accomplishing tasks to thinking more deeply about her growth in learning.

When I asked her what these questions did for her learning, she said, "They opened my eyes for what I need to do."

"They gave me a plan."

These questions provided her with a sense of accountability for her learning by focusing on what needed to take place for growth to occur. She started to identify other ways to assess her learning, such as filming herself to pinpoint areas of improvement. She was beginning to take control over her own learning; she was building her efficacy. This all started with clarity of learning from my instructional design, my teaching, and the culture I was establishing in my classroom.

Another important takeaway from this work was developing my students' competence across levels of complexity or learning levels (i.e., surface, deep, transfer). Prior to this professional learning experience, I wasn't structuring my teaching or supporting students in structuring their learning into these levels, and therefore, my learners did not understand the connection between various classroom activities. These levels of competency shifted the way I designed and taught each lesson as well as the way I designed my success criteria. I began the next term with learning intentions and success criteria that had surface, deep, and transfer levels and emphasized to the students the importance of surface-level knowledge in order to transfer.

As I am writing this, it is only Week 2 of the term; however, I am already beginning to see a change in the way students approach their tasks and projects because they know their surface and deep knowledge will eventually provide them with the ability to extend their ideas and transfer them into different contexts. They are developing their expertise.

—Bridget R. Mazzella
Inquiry Learning Team Leader
Xavier College, Llandilo
New South Wales, Australia

INTRODUCTION

"It makes no sense, unless you think back to Lawrence's long march across the desert to Aqaba. It is easier to dress soldiers in bright uniforms and have them march to the sound of fife and drum corps than it is to have them ride through the six hundred miles through snake-infested desert on the back of camels. It is easier and far more satisfying to retreat and compose yourself after every score—and execute perfectly choreographed plays—than to swarm about arms flailing, and contest every inch of the basketball court. Underdog strategies are hard."

—Gladwell, 2013

I walked into a classroom in September of 2017 and noticed a typical poster on the wall of Albert Einstein. This wasn't a particularly unique poster, but it stood out for me this time. The poster showed a headshot of Albert Einstein with the quote, *"Imagination is more important than knowledge."* I have seen this poster countless times, but on this day as I was observing students engaging in solving a problem that had not been solved by adults in the history of mankind, I was caught by how the teacher in the classroom was actualizing this adage in his teaching practices. The teacher was having students focus on their imaginations, and when needed, the students would search online or ask for the knowledge needed to make a case for their solution. The students were playing the part of experts working with others to create an elegant solution to the problem. The teacher was using an inquiry-based method to enable students to discover knowledge, explore solutions, and co-construct an approach to solving a real-life challenge.

It's tempting for teachers to try to create a classroom like this from the beginning and to want to treat their students as experts so early on in their learning. That is to bestow upon our youth the belief and expectation that they will solve the contemporary problems of the world, in class, today. First off, it seems to make intuitive sense that if students participate in activities that experts participate in, they will more likely become experts. Secondly, there is an element of empowering students to take ownership over their own learning that resonates with how adults feel about their own work experiences and how they would want to be treated as a child. As such, teachers look to find instructional methods that fit that paradigm.

Unfortunately, there is a major limitation to treating students like experts from Day 1 (or Day 417, as we will see later). How students think in their early years differs dramatically from how they think when they become experts (Willingham, 2010). Yes, that's right. They actually *can't* think like an expert (yet). We need to provide them with experiences that enable them to develop into experts while not expecting them to be experts right now. Moreover, we need to make sure that we show them we have high expectations and value them as learners while not requiring too much or too little from them as developing experts. This book provides a roadmap for navigating this demand.

> We need to provide students with experiences that enable them to develop into experts while not expecting them to be experts right now.

Accelerating Cognition: Developing Expertise Over Time

Ten thousand hours is the estimate of what it takes for someone to become an expert in a field. Ten thousand hours is the equivalent of 417 days or a little over nine years, if you were to devote approximately three hours to your craft per day (Gladwell, 2011). Unfortunately, this idea of time as the key or sole variable is incorrect. The literature actually shows that the "right" practice during those 10,000 hours is critical. As Ericsson and Pool (2016) argue, people must move beyond practicing a skill to engaging in deliberate and continuous practice during those 10,000 hours. If not, the result is people who are experienced but not necessarily experts.

So, what is the key differentiator of deliberate practice versus just practicing? For one, students need a clear sense of what strategies will enhance their learning as they move from understanding initial ideas to relating and transferring skills and ideas to different situations. Figure 0.1 illuminates these levels of complexity. Students must have a proportional level of understanding at surface, deep, and transfer to develop expertise.

To develop this level of understanding across surface, deep, and transfer levels, teachers need to anchor their instructional approaches to cognitive principles, such as the following:

- Students need to engage in practice over time to solidify understanding.

- Understanding begins with prior knowledge.

- Learning requires feedback and modeling from others.

- To learn, people need to understand expectations and current performance to reinvest in learning.

(McDowell, 2018)

Interestingly, there is recent research that illustrates that 10,000 hours of deliberate practice accounts for a relatively small amount (approximately 28%) of expertise and that 10,000 hours of deliberate

Figure 0.1   Levels of Complexity

Levels of Complexity	Description
Surface	I can define/label idea(s) or use skill(s) (but I can't connect the ideas and skills together)
Deep	I can relate idea(s) or connect skill(s) (but I can't apply the ideas and skills in different situations)
Transfer	I can apply idea(s) or skill(s) in different situations

experimentation leads to being a top expert (Simonton, 2011). The levels of complexity in Figure 0.1 show that both practice and experimentation are complementary and support novices in developing deeper learning through deliberate practice and then engaging in deliberate experimentation as they take their core knowledge and skills and transfer to authentic, real-world contexts.

Shared Learning: Developing Efficacy Over Time

In pursuing the development of student expertise, teachers must tackle the question of who bears the responsibility of such a task. Often the debate is on whether teachers control the learning of students or they empower students to take ownership over their own learning. Interestingly, these decisions actually come to the same conclusion—both fundamentally are related to teachers controlling the learning. If a teacher can empower (or give power to) a student, then they can also take away that power if needed. This false dichotomy also emerges in the debate over the roles of teachers: the "sage on the stage" or the "guide on the side." This debate often leads to the same type of messaging: "I, the teacher, gave you the opportunity to learn. You have to take that opportunity to learn or else."

I argue that to develop student expertise, the control over learning must be mutually shared between teachers and students. An effective way to move towards a shared responsibility of learning is for teachers to intentionally and consistently teach students how to build their efficacy in learning. Efficacy of learning may be best defined as a student's ability to take full responsibility over their own learning and support others in their pursuit of learning. Figure 0.2 breaks down efficacy into three key areas of focus for learners.

If a faculty engages in the process of developing a student's efficacy, then, over time, a student will develop the knowledge and skills necessary to navigate and lead their own learning. This starts with both teachers and students understanding students are not experts (yet) and that with time, the right interventions, and the right practice, students can build their efficacy and develop and sustain expertise. Moreover, teachers must understand that students require a strong relationship with teachers to develop as experts and that they must be taught content, tools, and strategies to be strong learners. Students will often make mistakes; they will need direct targeted feedback, and they will need to focus their energy and effort on how to improve

Figure 0.2   Areas of Focus—Efficacy of Learning

Areas of Focus	Description
Orientation	A student has a clear understanding of expectations, their current performance, and next steps to improve their learning. Orientation is governed by three essential questions: Where am I going? Where am I now? and What's next?
Activation	A student has a clear understanding of the dispositions and strategies necessary to improve their learning over time. Activation is anchored to the following key questions: What makes a strong learner? What do I do when I'm stuck in my learning? What strategies enhance my learning?
Collaboration	A student has a clear understanding of expectations and strategies to collaborate in groups or teams. Collaboration is anchored to the following key questions: How do I ensure that the feedback I'm giving and receiving is accurate? How do I support others in moving their learning forward? How can others strengthen and challenge my ideas?

over time. This sharing of learning puts teachers in an activator role, constantly assessing student performance and beliefs and taking an active step in supporting students emotionally and cognitively. Over time, students develop a more active role in their learning, developing individual and collective efficacy and expertise (i.e., developing surface-, deep-, and transfer-level knowledge).

> To develop expertise, the control over learning must be mutually shared between teachers and students.

Take Action: Implement the 5Cs Guiding Actions to Develop Student Expertise

How do we then develop a student's expertise and efficacy? Unfortunately, there are no magic potions to be found on your Twitter feed, but there are a lot of potions out there. In fact, since John Hattie's landmark *Visible Learning* research, educators have known that almost everything in education works. The question really comes down to what makes a substantial impact in building efficacy and expertise.

A few key actions have stood the test of time (see Figure 0.3). We should double down on such guiding actions and say "no" to the unsubstantiated fads of the day. Unfortunately, many of the guided practices shown in Figure 0.3 are not necessarily popular nor have they been perceived in the past to make much of a difference. Current hot topics such as creating better learning spaces, better curriculum, inquiry-based methods, giving over control of learning to students, optimal class sizes, changing our role to being facilitator teachers, or creating different class schedules in fact don't yield much of an impact on student learning or help build expertise (Hattie, 2009). These trends might be popular in the press and at school board meetings, but many of them fail to make a substantial impact on students.

The *Guiding Actions* in Figure 0.3 are in fact underdog strategies; the strategies that don't fit in with the current buzzwords or popular

Figure 0.3   The 5Cs: Guiding Actions for Developing Student Expertise

Clarify—Students must constantly know where they are going in their learning, where they are currently in their learning, and what next steps they need to take. Students should have a clear sense of varying levels of complexity in the core knowledge and skills they are working toward. Ideally, teachers use a variety of strategies to ensure learners have the ability to meet such learning requirements.

Challenge—Student prior knowledge is tested and then changed by identifying and describing ideas, comparing and contrasting ideas, and exploring contextual differences between problems. Teachers use various strategies to activate challenges and support learners in welcoming and meeting such challenges.

Check—Teachers are constantly checking in on learner progress toward curricular goals as well as learners' abilities to check their own understanding. This checking supports students and teachers in identifying next steps to improve learning.

Communicate—A plethora of research has articulated the amount of conversation that occurs amongst students regardless of a teacher's actions. Teachers use a variety of strategies to capitalize on the demands and attractiveness of socialization as well as the research on dialogue as a key factor in developing expertise.

Cross Contexts—Students must be able to address problems across contexts to meet transfer-level demands. Teachers support students in seeing similarities and differences between problems.

trends in education but actually are incredibly effective in building student expertise. Underdog strategies are built on the ideas that students are not experts (but they can be over time with the right interventions), that learning is anchored to fundamental principles of how the mind works, that students need to be involved in their learning with teachers, and that student thinking must be actively displayed in classroom activities so that the right interventions can move learning forward. Underdog education strategies have the ability to substantially promote meaningful learning and develop student expertise. Do we have the courage to say "no" to magic potions and stay focused on those strategies that are not very popular but make a huge impact on learning? If you do, then this is a book that will enable you to effectively and efficiently build student efficacy and expertise.

A Profile: An Efficacious and Expert Learner

Boser (2018) stated in his *Harvard Business Review* article entitled "Learning Is a Learned Behavior. Here's How to Get Better" that the ability to learn requires the cultivation of specific knowledge and skills through deliberate and intentional teaching. Boser (2018) goes further to state that educational institutions and companies don't focus much time on the idea of learning how to learn and this is an opportunity to fundamentally enhance the learning of children and adults. Figure 0.4 represents my attempt to illustrate a profile of the knowledge and skills learners must develop to become experts (surface, deep, and transfer) and efficacious (orientation, activation, and collaboration) in schools and careers.

Figure 0.4   The Efficacious and Expert Learner

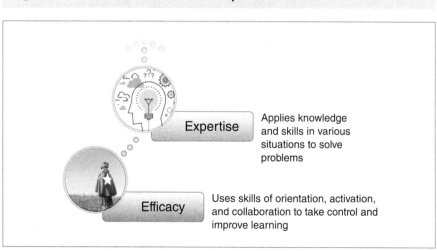

Efficacy icon: RichVintage/iStock.com; Experise icon: vasabii/iStock.com

An Example: Developing an Efficacious and Expert Learner

Imagine a young learner who is attempting to learn how to apply multiplication of fractions. In order to apply multiplication of fractions, this learner must first know how to multiply fractions and understand the definition of the multiplication of fractions. Furthermore, the learner must be able to justify and estimate the products of two fractions.

Figure 0.5 illustrates the goal of learning (i.e., learning intentions) and the expectations of meeting that goal (i.e., success criteria). Figure 0.6 illustrates the type of work that this learner may do to ensure an equal level of understanding at surface, deep, and transfer. At the surface level, the learner would calculate the product of $7/8 \times 1/3$. As the learner moves to the deeper level of understanding, they would justify the answer to $7/8 \times 1/3$ (this example illustrates the justification on a number line). The student would then apply their understanding in different contexts.

The path the learner can take to meet these expectations can vary. For example, the learner may first encounter the transfer-level problem and then, working with their teacher, develop surface and deep understanding to meet such a challenge. Regardless of the pathway, the teacher must work with the learner to provide the best interventions to serve the learner where they are in their learning.

This learner would go through this process over and over again, year after year, in every subject at school. As they learn surface, deep, and transfer expectations, their teachers would also be providing them with direct guidance on how they measure their own learning over time (i.e., orientation), how to apply strategies that enable them to continue to learn when they face setbacks (i.e., activation), and how they work with others to solve complex tasks (e.g., the dimensional analysis

Figure 0.5   Learning Intentions and Success Criteria

Learning Intention: I will apply multiplication of fractions		
Surface	**Deep**	**Transfer**
• Multiply fractions • Define multiplication of fractions	• Justify and estimate the products of two fractions	• Apply multiplication of fractions in different contexts

Figure 0.6 Example of Work

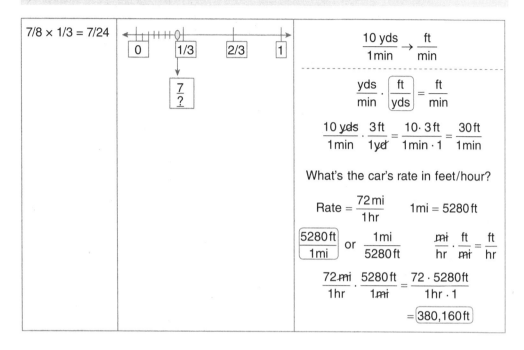

task in Figure 0.5) and give and receive feedback (i.e., collaboration). Over time, this learner would have the knowledge, skills, and dispositions to own their own' learning and have a robust understanding of core academic content.

After reading this book, you will be able to

Develop unit and lesson plan prototypes that maximize your impact on student learning while minimizing the amount of time you need to spend planning so that you can focus your time and energy on developing student expertise.

Implement classroom management strategies that enhance student individual and collective efficacy.

Align teaching practices to ensure students gain more in meeting core outcomes across levels of complexity (surface, deep, and transfer).

Support students at transfer-level learning by developing tasks, creating teams, and utilizing teaching strategies that move students to advanced levels of understanding.

Develop teacher collective efficacy to ensure that teachers use the most effective practices for advancing students and adult learning.

Special Features

- **5Cs:** The 5Cs provide a framework for teachers to develop a system of planning, classroom culture, and instructional approaches to advance student learning over time.

- **Researched-based strategies:** Each section of the book is thoroughly research based, providing multiple sources to substantiate the benefits and successful strategies of teachers and students.

- **Vignettes:** Educators who are interested in implementation can find valuable insights from the vignettes that illustrate where educational practitioners and students reflect on their experience teaching and learning in the classroom or provide concrete examples of how expertise and efficacy is developed over time.

- **Activities:** These will help you create your own next steps in designing plans, building a strong efficacious classroom culture and developing your instructional skills.

- **Examples, tables, checklists, protocols, rubrics, and images**: These facilitate understanding and application of the material.

- **Appendix:** The appendix offers resources mentioned in the book along with tools and exemplars for supporting teachers in their own practice.

- **Reflective questions:** Questions at the end of each chapter will assist you in thinking about how these strategies apply to your own teaching practices within your unique context and role.

- **Next steps:** Each chapter ends with Next Steps that encourage you to apply the content of each chapter to get you started in improving your teaching and learning practices.

Conclusion

This book is about the strategies teachers can use to ensure high levels of learning for every student. This outcome is reached by integrating the 5Cs Guiding Actions through unit and lesson planning, instruction, and cultural development. The book begins with an overview of the 5Cs Guiding Actions that enable teachers to illuminate the hidden lives of learners and develop expertise over time. Chapter 2 focuses on the classroom culture that ensures learners and teachers engage in the work of learning. Chapter 3 focuses on teacher preparations in unit and lesson design. Chapter 4 focuses on routines that teachers may use to intervene during classroom learning to most effectively support student learning. Chapter 5 focuses on developing collective teacher efficacy to continually monitor and support student efficacy and ultimately expertise. In the appendix, you will find several resources referenced throughout the book to help you accomplish these goals. Your major challenge throughout this book will be to focus on the 5Cs Guiding Actions and develop your own expertise. You will have to make a conscious decision to let go of practices that don't lead to developing student expertise. It is that simple and that hard.

REFLECTION QUESTIONS

1. What are your key takeaways from this chapter?

2. After reviewing the 5Cs, which one stands out for you? Why?

3. How do your students, colleagues, parents, and administration talk about depth of complexity (surface, deep, and transfer)? What steps are you going to take to begin discussing depth of complexity with learners?

4. How do your students, colleagues, parents, and administrators talk about student efficacy (orientation, activation, and collaboration)? What steps are you going to take to begin discussing a shared responsibility for developing student ownership over time with learners?

5. What steps could be taken to stay small and stay focused on a few initiatives that make a substantial impact?

6. What are key strategies that you, students, colleagues, parents, and administrators talk about in terms of making a substantial impact on student learning? What steps are you going to take to focus on learning in daily conversation and practice?

ACTIVITIES

ACTIVITY 0.1
OUR STORY OF EFFICACY AND EXPERTISE IN SCHOOL

Think through the story(ies) that permeates your classroom and your school about student efficacy and expertise. How would you describe a student developing expertise and efficacy in your school? How does this relate with the introduction of this book? What steps would you need to ensure that your narrative is of building student expertise and efficacy over time?

As a way of thinking about your story, ask yourself and your colleagues the following questions:

- How do our students learn?

- How do we talk about levels of complexity? Do we expect students to learn at each level? What levels do we prioritize?

- How do we teach at each level of learning? What does feedback look like at each level?

- How do students talk about their learning?

- How do we currently support our students in owning their own learning?

After discussing these questions, have the group read the introduction and Chapter I of this book and discuss the similarities and differences between what was discussed and what is presented in this book.

ACTIVITY 0.2
DEVELOPING A GRADUATE PROFILE FOR LEARNING

Find a small team of teachers and brainstorm the specific dispositions and skills you want to see from learners by the time they leave your grade level and/or school. Next read the introduction of this book and ask the team to highlight those dispositions and skills that are centered on efficacy and expertise.

Next present to the team the following question:

- Assume that students do not yet have the dispositions or skills you have listed. How would we ensure students learn these dispositions or skills in our grade level and/or school?

Have the team then brainstorm specific actions they could take in their planning, teaching, and classroom environment that would ensure (not just promote) students learn how to develop as experts.

ACTIVITY 0.3

EVIDENCE OF STUDENT EFFICACY

Find a small team of teachers and find out what students think about their own learning and how they focus on developing their expertise. From here, identify next steps to improve. One way to engage in this process is through "Learning Rounds." Please see the process below.

Learning Rounds

(Activity adapted from McDowell, *The Lead Learner*, 2018)

Guideline

- Speak to learners, listen to learners.
- Don't look at the adults (other than saying hello and goodbye).
- Provide your notes to the adults in the classroom (with no judgment).

Process

- Divide the questions below (see Figure 0.8) among a group.
  - The questions are based on orientation (a learner's ability to understand their performance and next steps relative to a goal), activation (a learner's belief in themselves to grow as a learner and a learner's actions in taking next steps), collaboration (a learner's ability to give and receive feedback), and relationships (a learner's perspective of the relationship with adults in the room).
- When you go into a classroom, write down only observations—What did you see or hear?
- After visiting several classrooms, find a place to meet together to discuss the observations, identify inferences, and determine next steps.

- Elect someone to jot down notes in the following table (Figure 0.7):
  - ○ Begin with writing down the observations (What?).
  - ○ Next, write down any inferences (So What?).
  - ○ Finally, write down potential suggested next steps (Now What?). Only provide next steps for those who were being observed if they are in the room and are actively participating. If they are not in the room, next steps should be directed toward those who were observing (i.e., What are our next steps?).

Figure 0.7   What? So What? Now What?

	What?	So What?	Now What?
Orientation			
Activation			
Collaboration			

Figure 0.8   Questions for Learning Rounds

#1 Orientation	#2 Activation	#3 Collaboration
• Where are you going in your learning right now? • What is your goal? • Where are you now in your learning? How do you know your performance level? • What next step do you need to take to improve your learning? • How do you improve your learning? How do you know if you are improving? • How will you know you learned something? • What do you need to do next in order to learn _____?	• What does a good learner look like in our class? • What happens if you make a mistake in your class? • Are you a good learner? Why or why not? • If you're not a good learner, can you become one? • What do the best learners in our class do differently from other learners? • How can you recognize the best learners in the class?	• How do you prefer to learn—on your own or with your peers? • Do you help others with their learning? How? • How do you know that the feedback you are giving is accurate? • How do you know the feedback you are receiving is accurate? • How do you feel about feedback? • How do you work with others to solve problems together? • How do you feel about being in teams or groups? Why?

#1 Orientation	#2 Activation	#3 Collaboration
• Do you understand how your learning is assessed? • Do you always know what you are learning and why? • What are you learning to do in art/health/math/English/science/etc., at the moment? How will you know when you have learned it? • How do you track your performance? • How do you talk about different levels of difficulty in learning? • What are the expectations at each level of complexity (surface, deep, transfer)? • Do I really get this idea? • Could I explain it to a friend? • What are my goals? • Do I need more surface level (or background) knowledge? • Do I need more practice? Do I need to practice differently?	• Are the best learners the same as the people who get the highest marks? • Should learning be easy or hard? Why? • What do you do when you get stuck? • What happens if you make a mistake in class? • What strategies do you use when you're lost? What do you do when you don't know what to do? • What strategies do you use when you're first learning something (surface)? • What strategies do you use when you're proficient (deep)? • What strategies do you use to go beyond or to apply your learning (transfer)? • What enables learners to persevere? • How do you learn? • What enables learners to recognize their successes and challenges? • What helps learners stay focused? • What strategies do you use when you're bored? Are you bored often?	• Are there any things that your peers could do to help you learn more? • Are there any things that you could do to help your peers learn more? • Can you tell me about a time when your peers really helped you learn something? • How can others push my thinking? • What feedback can I seek to improve my learning? • How can others strengthen or challenge my ideas? • How do I push someone's thinking forward without telling them what I want them to do? • How do we collectively press forward and co-construct new ideas and solutions? • How do we celebrate and challenge our individual ideas to create a better solution together? • How do I support others in pulling their thinking forward? • How do I pull someone's learning forward? • How do we pause our thinking and listen to others?

(Continued)

Figure 0.8   (Continued)

#1 Orientation	#2 Activation	#3 Collaboration
		• How do we pause on our first response and think deeply about supporting others? • How do we "stay soft on people and hard on content"? • What strategies do you use when you disagree? Or feel indifferent? • How do you support others in pulling their thinking forward? • How do you pull someone's learning forward?

Figure 0.9   Prompts for Discussion

What?	So What?	Now What?
• What did you notice about their understanding about where they were in their learning? • What did you notice about their ability to self-regulate their learning? • What did you notice about their attitudes toward getting something wrong or not understanding?	• What story are you telling yourself right now about these learners? What is another narrative we could be telling right now? • What inferences can we draw about student orientation, activation, and collaboration?	• In light of this data, what next steps can we take? • Who will do _____ (what) by when? • Do we need to stop doing something good to do these next steps? What will we stop doing?

What?	So What?	Now What?
• What did you notice about their feelings and ability to give and receive feedback? • What strategies emerged from learners in taking ownership over their own learning? • What stood out for you regarding student and teacher relationships?		

NEXT STEPS

• Ask colleagues to identify potential next steps they can take to maintain certain practices and change practices to improve learning.

	Current Practices	Next Steps
Practices to Maintain		
Practices to Change		

Chapter 1

GUIDING ACTIONS FOR EXPERTISE AND EFFICACY

Take a moment and ponder the following findings from Graham Nuthall's (2007) research on student learning:

- Eighty percent of what is happening in the classroom between and among students is largely hidden from teachers.

- Eighty percent of the information that students receive is from their peers.

- Eighty percent of that information received from peers is incorrect.

Just these three facts alone should cause educators to pause and think about what is happening in their classrooms on a daily basis. This is one of the reasons why formative assessment practices are so critical to the teaching and learning in a classroom. A teacher must constantly find out what students know and are able to do and then respond in the moment to effectively intervene. Moreover, a teacher must work with students to ensure each student is giving each other accurate information (Wiliam, 2011).

Research from Robert Marzano (2017), Hattie and Donoghue (2016), Hattie and Timperley (2007), and Fisher, Frey, and Hattie (2016) have all illustrated that, though almost every strategy makes an impact on learning, there are several strategies that have the highest probability of working at different levels of complexity (i.e., surface, deep, and transfer). That is, there are certain "best fit" strategies that seem to work best for learners when they are moving across each level of complexity (see Figure 1.1).

Figure 1.1   Best Fit Impact Model

	Surface	Deep	Transfer
Definition	Understand one concept, idea, and/or skill	Understand how concepts, ideas, and skills relate	Understand how to transfer concepts and relationships between concepts to various contexts
Anchor Strategies *Effective strategies for enhancing student learning at all levels of complexity*	**Student-Teacher Relationships**—*Teachers ensure that students have a safe and respectful environment and that all students know that teachers care about them personally and will do what it takes to ensure they get more than one year's growth in one year's time academically.* **Assessment Capable Learners**—*Teachers ensure that students can answer the following questions in class: Where am I going in my learning? Where am I now? What's next?* **Teacher Clarity**—*Teachers ensure that students are clear on the learning expectations of the class, unit, and lesson.* **Formative Evaluation**—*Teachers ensure that they and their students inspect their impact on learning and then take action to improve.*		
Best Fit Feedback Strategies *Effective forms of feedback to enable students to*	*As a means to acquire surface level knowledge . . .* • Distinguish between correct and incorrect information	*As a means to understand and develop deep understanding . . .* • Prompt others to detect errors in solutions	*As a means to transfer learning to other . . .* • Monitor and invest in seeking and acting on feedback to improve

	Surface	Deep	Transfer
move forward in their learning	• Prompt others to elaborate on information • Redirect others to paraphrase and offer examples	• Prompt others to articulate similarities and difference in concepts • Direct others to solve problems in multiple ways	• Prompt students to evaluate similarities and difference between problems
Best Fit Learning Strategies *Effective strategies students may use to assist them in their own learning*	*As a means to acquire information and discern between correct and incorrect learners . . .* • Outline • Use mnemonics • Summarize • Underline and highlight • Take notes • Engage in deliberate practice • Engage in rehearsal	*As a means to connect information and discern between correct and incorrect learners . . .* • Seek help from peers • Classroom discussions • Evaluation and reflection • Self-verbalization and self-questioning • Metacognitive strategies	*As a means to apply information and discern between correct and incorrect learners . . .* • Identify similarities and differences in problems • See patterns in new situations
Best Fit Instructional Strategies *Effective teaching strategies to enable students to develop understanding of core knowledge or skill*	*As a means to enable students to build surface knowledge and skill . . .* • Direct instruction • KWL chart • Advanced organizer	*As a means to enable students to build surface knowledge and skill . . .* • Jigsaw • Venn diagram • Socratic seminar • Number talks • Pair-share	*As a means to enable students to build transfer knowledge and skill . . .* • Problem and project-based learning • Discovery-based learning

Simultaneously, there are several strategies that are foundational or are "anchor" strategies that have a high impact across levels of complexity. For example, a student's relationship with a teacher is essential at all levels of understanding. Moreover, clarity of learning expectations and developing assessment capabilities are foundational skills that serve as a catalyst for current and future learning. Figure 1.1 provides a sampling of developing expertise-based strategies that teachers could use to support students in their learning journey.

If it is the case that the majority of the classroom is hidden from teachers, peer-to-peer information is prolific and inaccurate, and certain instructional, facilitative, and learning strategies are best used at the right level of learning, then teachers need new ways to design, implement, and manage learning in the classroom. In this chapter, we'll discuss the 5Cs Guiding Actions that enable educators to illuminate student learning, build students' capacity to build their own efficacy, and effectively intervene to develop student expertise. In short, this is accomplished by efficiently designing units and lessons, establishing practices to effectively intervene during class, and creating a classroom culture that enables all students to move from novices to experts.

The 5Cs: Guiding Actions for Developing Student Expertise

The 5Cs provide educators with a framework for how teachers and students should evaluate student learning in their classroom. Each guiding action is described in detail in Figure 1.2.

Clarify

When students clearly understand what the learning expectations are for them, their current performance, and what next steps they need to take, they have a much better chance of making decisions that will improve their own learning and thus take a greater level of responsibility over their learning. Moreover, when students have clarity over their learning, they tend to show substantial progress in their academic achievement. John Hattie's *Visible Learning* (2009) research, which has a cumulative sample size of over 500+ million students, shows that students can gain two

Figure 1.2   Students' and Teachers' Roles in Promoting the 5Cs

5Cs	Student Role	Teacher Role
Clarify	• Students learn how to clarify and assess where they are in their learning and articulate what next steps they need to take to improve. • Students have a clear sense of varying levels of complexity in the core knowledge and skills they are working toward.	• Teachers use a variety of planning and instructional strategies to help students clarify their stage of learning and to ensure learners have the ability to meet such learning requirements.
Challenge	• Students learn how to assess their prior knowledge and understand their misconceptions. • Students learn how to describe terms, identify relationships between ideas, and contextual differences between problems.	• Teachers use various strategies to prompt students to challenge their misconceptions, welcome such challenges as they learn, and identify and engage in learning at surface, deep, and transfer levels.
Check	• Students check on their progress and that of their peers.	• Teachers constantly check in on learner progress toward learning goals as well as learners' abilities to check their own understanding.
Communicate	• Students verify and improve their understanding through peer feedback, dialogue, and problem solving.	• Teachers capitalize on the prevalence of student socialization to help students develop expertise with the help of their peers.
Cross Contexts	• As students move to transfer they are able to address problems across contexts.	• Teachers support students in understanding similarities and differences between problems and addressing such problems.

years' worth of academic growth over one year's time when the following is true:

- They know where they are going in their learning (learning goals and success criteria);

- They know where they are currently in their performance; and

- They have a clear sense of next steps to move forward in their learning.

Moreover, when students know what is expected of them and understand the gap between those expectations and their current performance, feedback is far more effective (Hattie & Timperley, 2007). This is key, as the right type of feedback essentially doubles the rate of learning (Wiliam, 2011). We will discuss the right type of feedback in the next several chapters.

As such, the ability to clarify is a precursor to the high effect of feedback, the development of efficacy, and, in general, increased achievement. When students understand the expectations for their learning, they can more easily see the gap between those expectations and their own current performance. Then they may more readily understand why they need feedback and are presumably more apt to take and use the feedback to alleviate the discrepancy between expectations and current performance.

Challenge

In an interesting study in 2008, Muller looked into the efficacy of science videos on student learning. The research found that students outperformed their peers when they had to consciously think about their previous beliefs and understandings compared to new knowledge and ideas. In this study, Mueller argued that if previous ideas (that were often incomplete or incorrect) were not reviewed or challenged, new knowledge was not learned, and previous ideas—regardless of accuracy—were reinforced! As such, it is paramount that current thinking is analyzed, evaluated, and challenged against new ideas.

James Nottingham, in his 2017 book *The Learning Challenge*, called this dissonance between current understanding and aspiring knowledge a "cognitive wobble," referring to the notion of the struggle students have with determining whether new ideas can connect with previous ideas or if previous ideas must be replaced with new ideas.

The cognitive wobble can be caused by a number of different factors including the following:

- Confronting conflicting ideas (e.g., Idea I: Robin Hood steals from rich to give to the poor and is a hero; Idea 2: Stealing is bad.)

- Understanding and expanding our understanding of concepts (e.g., What is a prime number? What is justice?)

- Challenging prior knowledge (e.g., Students observe wind blowing through the trees and think that wind comes from trees.)

- Exploring paradoxes (e.g., To establish power, one must give power away.)

- Exploring the strengths and limitation of models and metaphors (e.g., Thinking of organizations like cellular organisms promotes the idea of unity and working together but may limit the notion and interest of conflict as an important aspect of organizational growth.)

The commonality here is that students must bring their prior knowledge and preconceived notions to their conscious mind and present them to others, against established criteria, and be ready and open to feedback and changing their mind. This is easier said than done. As Stephen Brookfield (1989) states, "Analyzing assumptions, challenging previously accepted and internalized beliefs and values, considering the validity of alternative behaviors or social forms—all these acts are at times uncomfortable and all involve pain" (125). Such is the nature of learning. Figure 1.3 illustrates two examples of requiring students to identify what they think and test that thinking against new knowledge or understanding.

> Students must bring their prior knowledge and preconceived notions to their conscious mind and present them to others, against established criteria, and be ready and open to feedback and changing their mind.

A key aspect of leveraging challenge is to encourage students to move through the cognitive wobble by providing surface-, deep-, and transfer-level strategies when the student needs it most. This requires teachers and students to have a clear understanding in the moment of where students are relative to expectations.

Figure 1.3   Activities That Link to Challenge

	Know	Need to Know
Surface		
Deep		
Transfer		
Other		

What I Now Know   What I Used to Think

$\longleftrightarrow$

What I Now Know   What I Used to Think

$\longleftrightarrow$

The "Know and Need to Know" activity articulates students prior knowledge (i.e., "know") and student current questions or struggles in their learning ("need to know"). Figure 1.3 provides students with an opportunity to place their "knows" and "need to knows" at level of complexity.

This document is helpful to teachers because they identify potential understandings and misunderstandings from the "know" column of the list. Moreover, teachers can identify what students are currently thinking they need to understand to meet the goals of learning (learning intentions and success criteria).

As students go through a learning experience, they may not intuitively notice how much they have improved in their thinking or how they have changed their thinking about concepts.

The "What I Know Now" and "What I Used to Think" process provides students with an opportunity to write down changes they have made between their current understanding and their previous understanding.

Testing and Challenging Prior Knowledge

When I'm stuck I . . .

When students are faced with information that is (a) brand new or (b) conflicting with prior ideas, they are more likely to be engaged in the content and, simultaneously, get stuck in their learning. They may lose confidence.

Step 1: Present misconceptions, paradoxes, metaphors, and different models to evoke dissonance in students understanding.

Step 2: Ask students to

- Write down how they feel
- What they will do to solve the problem that is presented to them
- Describe how they will maintain a level of optimism and confidence in their learning

Examples of misconceptions, paradoxes, metaphors, and models that you can present to your students include the following:

Cognitive Challenge Themes	Examples	Strategy to Progress
Paradoxes—*A contradictory statement that is true*	• The paradox of creativity is that the making of something new brings with it the destruction of something old. • Stealing is bad. Robin Hood is good.	• Frame situations in both/and vs. either/or. • Test assumptions and inferences to understand relationships between and among ideas.
Metaphor—*An approach to articulating a challenging idea simply*	• Students are told that the way in which cells work is much like how a city is run. • Students are told that one way to understand fractions is to cut a pizza.	• Test assumptions and inferences to understand the strengths and limitations of the metaphor. • Compare and contrast other metaphors. • Show students the content outside of the context.

(Continued)

(Continued)

Cognitive Challenge Themes	Examples	Strategy to Progress
General Models—*A way to articulate an idea or skill*	• Students are tasked with creating a model of DNA. • Students are tasked with developing a graph and ignoring certain variables.	• Test assumptions and inferences to understand the strengths and limitations of the metaphor. • Compare and contrast other metaphors. • Show students the content outside of the context. • Discuss with students limitations.
Misconceptions—*A misunderstanding of a concept or skill*	• Students see a student shooting a basketball and believe that more than one force is acting on the ball (assuming air resistance is a constant).	• Ask students to write down what they think they know and then test that knowledge after they receive new information. • Show students incorrect and correct examples and discuss the differences.
Perceived biases—*A persistent belief that has not been challenged by factual evidence*	• Students accept a stereotype of a particular subgroup or of themselves.	• Test assumptions and inferences to understand the intent behind such biases. • Provide concrete examples for challenging biases. • Provide examples for how perceived biases perpetuate (discuss limitations).

Check

Willingham (2010) once wrote that "memory is the residue of thought" (p. 41). The message he was trying to convey in his adage to educators was that what children thought about during an activity and throughout the day is what remains in their long-term memory. Though this information may appear intuitive or even trivial at first glance, research has shown that often the lives of teachers and students are associated with organizing and getting tasks complete. Teachers and students focus their mental efforts on completion of work, assigning points and grades, maintaining order, and accomplishing a series of tasks (Doyle, 1986; Nuthall, 2005). In fact, Nuthall (2001) found that students constantly compared how much they completed with that of other students and teachers spent a substantial amount of their time with students discussing resources, due dates, and next steps once tasks were completed. Conversations about learning—that is, conversations about prior knowledge relative to a specific learning outcome—were absent or minimal in the classroom (see Activity 1.3 for a detailed example).

Andrea Coffey, Lead Teacher
Anglo-American School
Moscow, Russia

The concept of distinguishing learning intentions and success criteria from contexts and tasks is at the heart of ensuring students know what to focus on in their learning. This was a significant realization for our faculty—including me! Separating the learning intention from the activity is what makes learning transferable to so many situations; students leave our classrooms as empowered thinkers, determining the most effective way to solve real-life challenges.

This progressive shift in thinking addresses the age old question, "Why are we learning this?" Students understand why they are learning something when they see it as relevant across different facets of their lives. For teachers, this shift emphasizes what is *most* important: the learning intentions and success criteria. Prioritizing these rather than the context and task ensure clarity for students, as they will understand what they are trying to learn and how they will know they have learned it rather than what they need to do to be successful on a specific assessment. This helps teachers streamline the planning process, so they can spend time developing engaging lessons that get at the core of the learning intentions.

Moreover, as we discussed in the last section, "Challenge," students often bring incomplete or incorrect knowledge to their work, which must be recognized by both teachers and students to improve.

This requires teachers, individual students, and peers to constantly check on student thinking to clarify student focus on learning goals, understand current performance, and provide instruction and feedback that instigates and then resolves the cognitive wobble. Figure 1.4 shows an example of how one elementary class uses cups to easily check where students are in their learning journey.

Communicate

As discussed previously, left to their own devices, students often reinforce or advocate ideas that are incorrect or incomplete (Nuthall, 2007). However, research indicates that when guided by a teacher,

---

Figure 1.4   Checking in Elementary Example

The following image depicts an activity in which students use colored cups to symbolize their level of understanding of the core content being explored in the classroom. The green cups stand for "comfortable" with the material, yellow stands for "learning" the material, and red means "struggling" with the material. This process is a simple and quick way of assessing student performance.

Source: Ross School; Ross, CA. Used with Permission.

Figure 1.5   Check-In/Room for Improvement Protocol, High School Example

The following high school example illustrates a process by which students review their work and identify the rationale for their performance and next steps they may take to enhance their learning.

> Conversations about learning—that is, conversations about prior knowledge relative to a specific learning outcome—were absent or minimal in the classroom.

CHECK-IN: Where am I? Where do I want to be?

High School Example

R2 GRADE: _____

Top 2 Writing Scores: **(Name of Assignment + Score)**

_____

Top 2 Reading Scores: **(Name of Assignment + Score)**

_____

Writing: I am making progress . . .	Writing: I am still struggling with . . .
Reading: I am making progress . . .	Reading: I am still struggling with . . .
Work habits that help me . . . (some examples: seeks feedback, apply effort and practice, constantly strives for personal best, carves out time for homework, focuses during class time, unplugs from technology when reading, etc.)	What obstacles are in my way? Are there any habits inhibiting my learning?
I need teacher support on . . .	I would like an opportunity to . . .

Source: Mall, J. San Anselmo, CA

peer influences (including assisting others with their work, tutoring, giving feedback, and providing social support) can yield a substantial impact on student learning (Hattie, 2009).

Developing skills in classroom communication is essential because, even when it is done, the research shows that communication is executed unsuccessfully. The research shows that both teachers and students have difficulty discussing student performance (McDowell, 2009) and that classroom discussions often involve inadequate reasoning that result in faulty conclusions (Ochoa & Robinson, 2005). Classroom group discussions can be problematic in that the members often fail to constructively negotiate opinions and rarely arrive at a shared understanding or solution (Ochoa, Kelly, Stuart, & Rogers Adkinson, in press). One study involved teachers who supported peer-to-peer feedback but did not exhibit the actual behaviors that prompted and leveraged cognitive conflict—nor did they consistently check on student learning and provide interventions on issues related to learning (McDowell, 2009). However, there are ways to promote, leverage challenge, and consistently check within classroom routines that enable students and peers to focus on, talk about, and take action on learning. For example, Figure 1.6 illustrates a pre-assessment and post-assessment of a student's writing in which the student's writing expressed a higher degree of detail in the second draft than the pre-assessment. The change in detail was due to the teacher providing the students detailed success criteria, exemplars, and for students to give and receive feedback with peers. Throughout this book, you will find strategies and guides for how to communicate more effectively in the classroom.

Cross Contexts

One of the key aspects of developing expertise is to use surface and deep knowledge and skills in application-based (or transfer-level) situations. Hattie and Donoghue (2016) argue that providing cognitively challenging tasks to students is an effective way to support students to develop their knowledge and skills at the transfer level. In *Rigorous PBL by Design* (McDowell, 2017), I argue for designing problems or projects that require students to learn core content and skill knowledge at surface and deep levels and then apply that knowledge to problems that are contextually based. For example, let's say students were required to define (surface) food chains and relate (deep) them to food webs in order to hypothesize (transfer) why the reintroduction of sea otters in the North Pacific Ocean would influence the natural balance of the ecosystem. Even more, we could require students to hypothesize what would happen across different contexts (e.g., the golden eagles in the Altamont Pass, the gray wolves in

Figure 1.6   Class Feedback

The following example illustrates a pre- and post-assessment of a student's writing. The pre and post occurred within the same day of class. In the first assessment, the student was given general directions on writing an opinion piece. In the first draft, students mention how they like horses and would prefer to visit a farm. After writing the initial draft, the entire class was shown the piece of writing, success criteria, and then asked to give feedback to enhance their writing. The post assessment shows the change in the writing over a short amount of time. Specifically, the student provides descriptive language and a formal format to persuade others, such as "Imagine a beautiful horse galloping gracefully in a field." The second draft also adds specific rationale, "Riding is fun because you can feel the wind in your hair," and the draft describes different gaits a horse rider can experience. The first draft says it's fun to visit a farm, but with the introduction of success criteria, the second draft includes rationale for why it is fun to visit a farm and adds imagery and a greater level of detail.

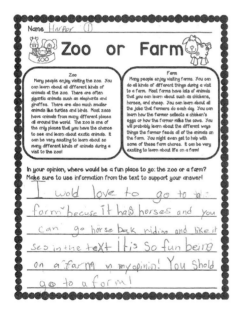

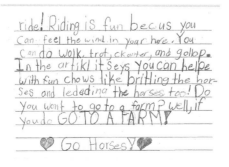

Source: J. Gomez, personal communication, 2018

Figure 1.7   Sample Learning Intentions and Success Criteria

Learning Intentions—*what are the goal(s) for learning*		
• I will develop a model to describe the movement of matter among plants, animals, decomposers, and the environment.		
Step 2: Success Criteria—*how student success is gauged*		
Surface	**Deep**	**Transfer**
Students will . . .	Students will . . .	Students will . . .
• Define food chains, food webs, ecosystems • Describe a healthy ecosystem • List types of organisms (producers, consumers, decomposers) • Describe introduction and reintroduction of a species	• Relate food chains and food webs • Relate types of organisms and their role in food chains and food webs • Relate introduction or reintroduction to the balance of ecosystems • Relate the complexity of food chains/webs to the health of an ecosystem	• Apply the concept of reintroduction to the health of an ecosystem into unique contexts

New Mexico, the elephants in Kenya, the wild horses of Assateague). A key element of developing expertise is for students to move from surface to deep and to transfer. These types of problems and situations enable them to begin to apply their knowledge to their discipline (and other disciplines) and begin to participate in processes similar to experts. In the following chapters, educators are provided with tools for how to teach to transfer for every learner.

Putting Principles of Expertise Into Practice Successfully

How can we take these 5Cs Guiding Actions and translate them into our planning, teaching, and classroom culture? Figure 1.9 lays out success criteria for teacher actions that will ensure students are learning at high levels. The remaining chapters of the book provide guidance and examples in these areas.

Figure 1.8   Transfer Task Scenarios

Scenario I: Golden Eagle Reduction	Scenario II: Sea Otters Repopulation
In the following scenario, students are tasked with applying the learning intention and success criteria presented in Figure 1.7. In this problem, students are tasked with finding a solution to preventing further golden eagle deaths due to the increase in wind turbines in their home range.	In the following scenario, students are tasked with applying the learning intention and success criteria presented in Figure 1.7. In this problem, students are tasked with finding a solution to reintroducing the sea otter to the Pacific Ocean.

Source: Kmatija/iStock.com	*Source:* GomezDavid/iStock.com

Figure 1.9   Success Criteria for Developing Student Efficacy and Expertise

	Planning *Chapter 2*	Culture *Chapter 3 and Chapter 6*	Teaching *Chapter 4 and Chapter 5*
Clarify	• Establishes learning intentions and success criteria across surface, deep, and transfer levels. • Learning intentions and success criteria are void of contexts, tasks, and activities.	• The focus of the classroom is on student growth, both in the areas of expertise (surface, deep, and transfer) and efficacy (orientation, activation, and collaboration).	• Clear expectations for student learning at the beginning of the unit and lesson are provided. • Routines are in place to support students in answering the questions, *Where am I going? And Where am I now?*

(Continued)

Figure 1.9   (Continued)

	Planning *Chapter 2*	Culture *Chapter 3 and Chapter 6*	Teaching *Chapter 4 and Chapter 5*
• **Challenge**	• Tasks and lessons are aligned to surface, deep, and transfer expectations. • Instructional, feedback, and learning strategies are aligned to surface, deep, and transfer expectations.	• Conversations are focused on discussing and taking action on meeting learning demands.	• Lessons are provided at appropriate levels of complexity. • High probability strategies are used in lessons to meet student needs.
• **Check**	• Units and lessons plan for student prior knowledge and core content knowledge.	• Everyone inspects their impact and that of others.	• Routines enable students to identify, test, and discuss prior knowledge relative to key outcomes. • Lesson stops, randomizers, and pair-share are used to identify student performance.
Communicate	• Lessons specifically plan for student dialogue and ensuring students spend time on evaluating their performance, giving and receiving feedback, and discussing content and solving problems.	• Consistent routines are established to ensure students inspect their progress, give and receive feedback, and solve complex problems collectively.	• Protocols are in place to support students in giving and receiving feedback, discussing content, and solving problems.

	Planning *Chapter 2*	Culture *Chapter 3 and* *Chapter 6*	Teaching *Chapter 4 and* *Chapter 5*
Cross Contexts	• Units are designed so that students are engaged in cognitively challenging tasks at the transfer level that extend beyond one context.	• Problem-solving processes are adopted to solve complex tasks.	• Routines are in place to ensure students meet transfer-level requirements.

Conclusion

The research shows that we need to illuminate student thinking in the classroom and provide accurate interventions (instruction, feedback, and learning strategies) at their level of learning (surface, deep, and transfer). As discussed in the Introduction, students must progress through each of these levels of learning to develop their expertise over time. Moreover, students need to develop their efficacy (orientation, activation, and collaboration) to sustain the journey toward expertise over time. The 5Cs guide educators toward selecting the right strategies to move learning forward and ultimately build student expertise.

Teachers must focus their efforts on eliciting students' understanding and supporting students in developing strategies to change their understanding or further extend their understanding. To do this, teachers need to develop a series of practices that elicit student understanding, provide appropriate responses to learners, develop a cadre of strategies to support each student, and develop the means for constantly inspecting teacher efficacy in relation to student learning.

The remaining chapters of this book bring these guiding actions to life with practical steps and vivid examples for developing student expertise. Next, Chapter 2 lays out a process for establishing an efficacious culture.

REFLECTION QUESTIONS

- How do you currently leverage the 5Cs in your practice?

- How do the 5Cs relate to developing student expertise? How have your practices in the past reflected these messages? What evidence do you have that supports your answers to the first two questions? What changes do you think need to happen in your practice?

- What appears to be your key "need to knows" or questions as you move to the next several chapters?

- After reviewing the instructional, feedback, and learning strategies, what aspects of the "anchor" strategies and "best fit" strategies resonate? What challenges your thinking for supporting students as they move from surface, deep, and transfer?

ACTIVITIES

ACTIVITY 1.1
5CS PROFICIENCY ASSESSMENT

In a meeting with your colleagues, conduct an assessment of your individual proficiency in clarifying, challenging, checking, communicating, and crossing contexts with students. Ask each team member to discuss his or her proficiency of these 5Cs in terms of planning, culture, and teaching. Use the success criteria outlined in Figure 1.9 to help guide your discussion.

Step 0 (before the meeting): Collect evidence of the 5Cs to bring to the meeting. Team members can self-assess the degree to which each Guiding Action is part of their practice Figure 1.10.

- Bring data to the meeting that represent the 5Cs in their practice.

- Bring data to the meeting that represent the 5Cs in the actions of students.

Step 1: Discussion. As a group, discuss the evidence you've collected and how it can help determine proficiency in the 5Cs.

Step 2: Assessment. Use Figure 1.11 to rate your proficiency on each of the 5Cs regarding your teaching practice.

Which guiding actions are a consistent part of your practice?

Which guiding actions are not part of your practice?

Step 3: Action Plan. Team members determine individual and/or collective next steps to improve. I recommend using a Charette Protocol, such as Figure 1.12, to conduct this feedback process. You can also use other protocols, such as Resource 6.1 The Critical Friends Protocol.

Figure 1.10   Evidence of Implementation

5Cs	I have collected several pieces of evidence to determine the degree to which I have met established success criteria.	I have collected limited evidence to determine the degree to which I have met established success criteria.	I have no evidence to determine the degree to which I have met established success criteria.
Clarify	Example: *I have asked students a series of questions about their clarity in learning (one example is data collected from the Learning Rounds process).*	Example: *I have asked a few students questions about their efficacy, expertise, and learning (one example is data collected from the Learning Rounds process).*	Example: *I do not currently have data regarding student clarity.*
Challenge			
Check			
Communicate			
Cross Contexts			

Figure 1.11   5Cs Guiding Actions Self-Assessment

5Cs Rating Scale

−1 = Not a part of my practice

0 = Occasionally part of my practice but not consistent

1 = Main focus, consistent part of my practice

	Planning	Teaching	Culture
Clarify	−1--------0--------+1	−1--------0--------+1	−1--------0--------+1
Challenge	−1--------0--------+1	−1--------0--------+1	−1--------0--------+1
Check	−1--------0--------+1	−1--------0--------+1	−1--------0--------+1
Communicate	−1--------0--------+1	−1--------0--------+1	−1--------0--------+1
Cross Contexts	−1--------0--------+1	−1--------0--------+1	−1--------0--------+1

Figure 1.12   Charette Feedback Process

The following protocol is designed to provide students and educators with specific feedback regarding a product, presentation, or process. The protocol is typically used when an individual or team has reached a point in a process of development in which they cannot easily move forward on their own. Typically the presenter is looking for feedback around the following two questions: How can I/we make our work better? What is our next step(s) to improve our work?

20–40 minutes

Opening Moves (Introduction) (5 minutes)

- Review purpose of protocol
- Review agreements (or norms) of the team
- Identify facilitator/participant and presenter
- Review success criteria of product, process, or presentation being evaluated

Opening Presentation (5 minutes)

- The teacher(s) or student(s) requesting feedback provides a 3-minute overview on the product, process, or presentation.
- The presenting teacher, teacher team, student, or student team will then provide the specific question(s) they are looking for from the participants.
- The presenter will provide answers to any clarifying question (1–2 minutes).

Discussion

- The participants then discuss the questions provided by the presenter. These may include strengths, questions, and suggested next steps. There are no hard and fast rules here other than that the presenter must listen.

- Once the presenter has heard what they need to hear, they may stop the process by saying, "Thank you. I have the feedback I/we need to move forward."

Closing Remarks

- The facilitator thanks the groups and debriefs the process.

ACTIVITY 1.2
IDENTIFY YOUR BEST FIT IMPACT MODEL

As a team, identify the strategies you believe constitute the best instructional, learning, and feedback strategies for learners at surface, deep, and transfer as well as the core anchor strategies for learners.

Figure 1.13 illustrates a simplified example of what the model may look like. Figure 1.14 provides an example of one instructional, learning, and feedback strategy for each level of complexity.

Figure 1.13   Best Fit Impact Model Example

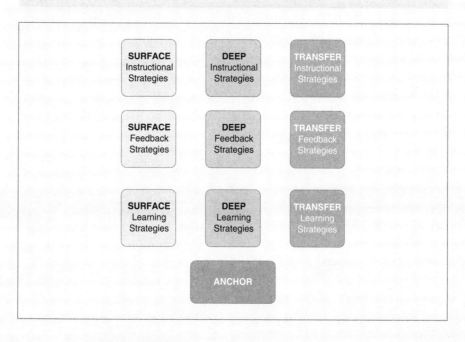

Figure 1.14 provides specific strategies teachers may use at surface, deep, and transfer levels of learning, along with key strategies (i.e., anchor) that should be universally applied across all levels of complexity. For example, direct instruction (instructional strategy), deliberate practice (learning strategy), and elaboration (feedback strategy) are effective strategies at the surface level of learning. Deep learning is best leveraged with strategies such as Socratic seminar (instructional strategy), self-questioning (learning strategy), and detecting our own errors (feedback). Transfer is leveraged with inquiry-based methodologies such as problem-based learning (instructional strategy), analyzing patterns (learning strategy), and monitoring performance (feedback strategy). These strategies are complemented by anchor strategies that include strong teacher-student relationships, collective efficacy of teachers (see Chapter 5), development of students' assessment capabilities (see Chapter 2), teacher clarity (see Chapter 3), and teacher inspection of their own performance (i.e., formative evaluation).

Figure 1.14   Best Fit Impact Model Example

Best Fit Impact Model		
Surface	**Deep**	**Transfer**
Direct Instruction	Socratic Seminar	Problem-based learning
Deliberate practice	Self-questioning	Analyzing patterns
Elaboration	Error detection	Monitoring performance
Student teacher relationships		
Collective efficacy		
Assessment capable learners		
Teacher clarity		
Formative evaluation		

ACTIVITY 1.3

CHECKING THE CULTURAL MYTHS AND REALITIES OF THE CLASSROOM

Step 1: Read the excerpt from Graham Nuthall's (2005) *The Cultural Myths and Realities of Classroom Teaching and Learning.* Use your SMART phone or tablet to click on the QR code below. Scroll to the bottom of page 926 (page 32 out of 40 of the pdf). The excerpt begins, "Let me finish by describing a teacher who has attempted to step outside the standard routines of teaching and create a new kind of classroom . . ." and ends on page 928 (p. 34 out of 40) with the sentence, "Such is the power of culture and the routines and myths by which teachers structure and understand daily life in their classrooms . . ."

Step 2: Discuss in small groups.

Step 3: Answer the following questions:

- From your reading of Nuthall's, *The Cultural Myths and Realities of Classroom Teaching and Learning* excerpt, describe how assumptions about students impact student learning and classroom instruction.

- How can we use the 5Cs to challenge these myths?

- Specifically, how does "Check" enable us as teachers to challenge our thinking?

Graham Nuthall Excerpt

http://bit.ly/ NuthallExcerpt

To read a QR code, you must have a smartphone or tablet with a camera. We recommend that you download a QR code reader app that is made specifically for your phone or tablet brand.

NEXT STEPS

- Discuss the key takeaways from this chapter.

- Have your department go through the Reflection Questions and Activities sections and map out potential next steps in implementing the 5Cs.

- Have staff identify next steps to improve the team's collective work in developing student expertise.

Chapter 2

CONDITIONS FOR IMPACT

Creating a Culture of Collective Efficacy

Figure 2.1 provides a glimpse into the expectations for learners in Mrs. Gomez's classroom (we will use the term learners as a substitute for students throughout this chapter). In Mrs. Gomez's classroom, a key outcome for learners is to know the outcomes of learning, to think about their current performance, and to identify next steps to improve their learning. In her class, one of the most important goals is for students to progress in their learning. This requires students to have a clear sense of direction in their learning (i.e., they know where they are going, where they are, and what's next), a core set of beliefs and behaviors that enables them to prevail when they struggle in their learning, and a core set of strategies to work with their peers to enhance learning for all. Students in this class are a part of a culture that invites all students into developing efficacy in their learning, sharing in the responsibility of growth in learning for others, and developing expertise. This chapter walks through the steps necessary to create a culture that integrates collective efficacy and expertise over time.

Figure 2.1   Progress and Proficiency Cue for Learners

Source: Photo courtesy of J. Gomez and Maxine Mannion, personal communication, 2017

Culture of Learning

A culture may be best defined as the way in which a group of people solve problems. As groups of people work through recurring problems, they develop a series of beliefs, values, assumptions, and common processes and strategies to work through said tasks. Over time, these beliefs, values, assumptions, and processes become less overt and part of "the way we do business here." When people attempt to change culture or "the way we do business here," they often focus on changing the values, assumptions, beliefs, processes, and strategies. But in fact the way to understand how a culture is perpetuated and how a culture changes is to focus on recurring problems that the culture solves. As Christensen and Shu (2006) argue, "When attempting to change an organization's culture, in other words, the fundamental unit of analysis, or the starting point, is the *task* [problem], not the process or culture—because processes, priorities and culture are a *response* to recurring tasks [problem]."

In this way, it is important to reflect on the problems or tasks that students and teachers are routinely addressing in the classroom. Are the recurring tasks or problems we are attempting to solve each day focused on proficiency and appropriate behavior? Classrooms that share in the task of appropriate behavior and proficiency develop shared learning experiences that focus on proficiency (e.g., *Did I get an A? Why didn't I get an A? What did you get?*) and staying out of trouble (e.g., I need to sit on the rug, I need to raise my hand to go to the bathroom, I put the homework in this bin or I get a zero).

Some classrooms have problems that are oriented toward progress (e.g., *Am I improving? How did I improve? What has been helpful for you during this unit?*) and focusing on enhancing interactions between each other (e.g., *What about my idea connects to your idea? How would you improve my work? Here is one suggestion to move your learning forward*). You can identify the types of problems that your students face and routinely address by reflecting on the following questions:

- How do your students define a good learner? How would they compare a strong learner to a struggling learner?

- How do they view challenge?

- How do your students define success in your classroom?

- How do your students feel about sharing their successes and challenges in class? How would they share those successes with others?

- What would students say about what they spend the majority of their time on?

- What do students say when you ask them where they are going in their learning?

- What do students say when you ask them where they are in their learning and what next steps they need to take?

- What would they say are the outcomes of learning in your classroom?

Additionally, consider your own role as an educator by asking yourself questions such as the following:

- What does a good student look like to you?

- What is your role and responsibility in the classroom?

- Who is responsible for the learning in the classroom?

- What recurring problems do you have students engage in?

- What recurring problems do you engage in?

Recurring Problems

There may be several types of school cultures, but for the purposes of this book, I will highlight two main types: (1) compliance culture and (2) learning culture. In a compliance culture, the recurring problems of classrooms are oriented toward staying out of trouble, getting good marks, getting assignments done (e.g., worksheets, projects, products), and comparing student performance to that of their peers. This occurs in every type of environment, from strictly traditional, tightly controlled classrooms to inquiry-based 21st Century classrooms. The processes, environment, and assumptions may look different, but the recurring problems in these classrooms are the same: Stay out of trouble, get an A, get work done, do better than the person next to you. You can visit a variety of classrooms and think you are seeing different cultures, but what you are really seeing is a common attitude focused on compliance.

In a learning culture, recurring problems are not focused on compliance. Instead, educators and students are focused on growth in academic proficiency across surface, deep, and transfer levels of learning as well as developing individual and collective efficacy of the entire class. As such, teachers can make a monumental impact on how students make the change toward progress by first articulating to students that the tasks of the classroom are the following:

- Developing expertise—ensuring more than one year's growth in one year's time across levels of complexity (surface, deep, and transfer)

- Developing efficacy—using strategies that enable learners to take control over their own learning and supporting the learning of others in the classroom

Teachers can identify the current status of the classroom's focus on expertise by completing the checklist in Figure 2.2. Expertise-based practices described in the Developing Expertise Checklist will be described in further detail in the remaining chapters.

One way to gather data on efficacy is to conduct learning rounds in your classroom (see Activity 0.3). The rest of this chapter looks at other forms of evidence collection for developing efficacy and strategies that can be embedded in the culture of the classroom to improve individual and collective efficacy of students and ultimately expertise in learning.

Figure 2.2 Developing Expertise Checklist

Teacher	Learner
☐ Establishes a common set of metrics to describe one year's growth in one year's time as well as the determination of proficiency with learners	☐ Routinely uses pre-assessments at all levels of complexity to measure current knowledge and adapt learning strategies to improve
☐ Ensures reporting systems are directly aligned with growth and proficiency expectations	☐ Routinely reflects on pre-assessment, "just in time" assessments, and post-assessment at all levels of complexity data to measure performance and determine next steps
☐ Routinely uses pre-assessments, "just in time" assessments, and post-assessments at all levels of complexity to measure learners' current knowledge and adapt instruction	☐ Routinely reflects on progress toward meeting learning intentions and success criteria and identifying strategies to improve
☐ Routinely shares pre-assessment and post-assessment at all levels of complexity data with learners to measure and discuss proficiency and progress and co-construct next steps	☐ Routinely visualizes current understanding and articulates next steps
☐ Routinely has learners reflect on their progress toward meeting learning intentions and success criteria and identifying strategies to improve	☐ Routinely gives and receives feedback to improve learning for themselves, peers, and the teacher
☐ Routinely visualizes learners' current understanding and shares next steps with others	
☐ Routinely gives and receives feedback to improve learning of students and colleagues	

Defining Efficacy

As discussed in the introduction of this book, for a learner to take action over their learning, they must be able to exhibit the three key areas of efficacy. They must be able to

- **Orient** their learning: know where they are going in their learning, where they are in their learning, and what next steps they need to take to improve their learning

- **Activate** their learning: know what makes a great learner, what strategies move their learning forward, and how to persevere when they get stuck, bored, or don't care about the subject

- **Collaborate** with others: know how to give feedback that moves learning forward, how to receive feedback, and how to work with others to solve complex tasks

Evidence of Efficacy

To begin developing a culture that develops learner individual and collective efficacy, one must first gather evidence of efficacy in the classroom. One way to do this is to ask learners a series of questions associated with the three key areas of efficacy (i.e., orientation, activation, and collaboration). The following subsections describe each area of efficacy and provide a series of questions to ask learners. From this data, there are a number of ways to enhance individual and collective efficacy, which will be explored later in this chapter.

Orientation

Orientation is defined as a learner's ability to clarify expectations of learning (i.e., learners can answer the following question: Where am I going in my learning?), their current performance toward those expectations (i.e., learners can answer the following: Where am I now in my learning?), and understand their tentative next steps in learning

Figure 2.3   Learning Culture Focus Areas

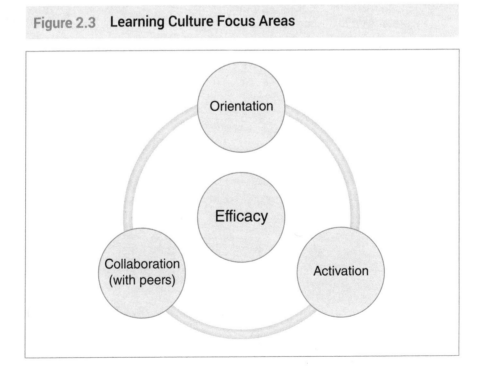

(i.e., learners can answer the question: What's next?). These behaviors allow learners to understand expectations of learning and their performance and identify and act upon data that drives next steps in the learning process. A preponderance of research has articulated the ability of students to be assessment capable as one of most successful strategies to enhance student learning (Hattie, 2009; Wiliam 2011).

Figure 2.4 illustrates a series of questions that teachers may use to identify a student's orientation toward monitoring, evaluating, and improving their own learning. As we will see in Chapter 4, these questions must be continually juxtaposed with content-based instruction from teachers. Often students' minds focus on the task and the context of learning rather than the content knowledge and skills that they are supposed to be learning through a task and through a context (McDowell, 2017). To develop mastery, teachers must continually bring a student's mind back to how they are progressing in their learning.

Activation

Stonefields School in Auckland, New Zealand, articulates the following quality of a learner on their website (Stonefields Schools, 2018):

The focus on developing learners' capacity to thrive in tricky situations—knowing what to do when they don't know what to do—is valued highly. Teachers explicitly teach learners strategies to get out of "I'm stuck" situations. Being stuck is celebrated and harnessed as an opportunity to build each individual's learning capacity.

Figure 2.4 Key Questions to Assess Students' Orientation Efficacy

Orientation Criteria	Key Questions
Clarity of Learning Expectations	• Where am I going in my learning? • What does success look like at the end?
Depth of Complexity	• What are the expectations at each level of complexity (surface, deep, transfer)?
Inspecting Performance	• Where am I in my learning? • Am I currently being challenged in my learning? • How have I improved? • Where are areas of growth for me in meeting expectations?
Charting the Way	• What next steps can I take to meet the learning expectations?

Activation may be best defined as a set of beliefs and related actions that students utilize when they are faced with "tricky situations." To be *active*, one must know what makes a strong learner and have a set of strategies that enables them to approach new problems, handle failure, persist, and reflect on their learning. Ross School in Northern California uses a series of prompts to prime students' thinking about their dispositions (i.e., beliefs and perspectives) and the strategies they use when they are stuck in their learning (see Figure 2.5).

Figure 2.5   Poster: Who Am I as a Learner?

WHO AM I AS A LEARNER?

HOW AM I LEARNING?	DO I BELIEVE IN MYSELF?	CAN I GIVE AND RECEIVE FEEDBACK?	WHAT'S MY RELATIONSHIP LIKE WITH MY TEACHER?
• Where are you now in your learning?	• What does a good learner look like?	• Do you help others with their learning?	• Does your teacher help you understand what you're learning? How?
• What's your goal?	• What happens if you make a mistake?	• How do you accept feedback?	• Does your teacher clearly explain what you need to do to make progress in your learning?
• Where are you going?	• What do you do when you get stuck?	• How do you work with others to solve problems together?	
• What next steps do you need to take to improve?	• What strategies do you use when you're lost?	• What feedback can I seek to improve my learning?	• Does your teacher help you with "how" to learn and "what" to learn?
• How do you know if you're learning or improving?	• What strategies do you use at surface, deep, and transfer levels?	• How do you know that the feedback you are giving and receiving is accurate?	
• What are the expectations at surface, deep, and transfer levels?	• How do you persevere?		

Source: Ross School; Ross, CA. Used with Permission.

Schools such as Reese Elementary School in Sacramento, California, have developed a series of dispositions to develop the appropriate mindset for tackling challenging tasks, including learn from mistakes, never give up, effort matters, and reach for goals. Beyond beliefs, students must also possess a set of strategies to handle "tricky situations." Eduardo Briceño (2015) argues that, "students often haven't learned that working hard involves thinking hard, which involves reflecting on and changing our strategies so we become more and more effective learners over time, and we need to guide them to come to understand this" (para. 5). Examples of these strategies can be seen in Figures 2.6, 2.7, and 2.8.

Figure 2.6 includes images from Stonefields School that promote desirable learner dispositions, such as questioning, being determined, being self-aware, and reflecting on learning.

Figure 2.7 shows a poster from Reese Elementary identifying how visible learners ask questions, evaluate work based on success criteria, receive and respond to feedback, and state what they are learning.

The Where Am I in My Learning reference post from the Ross School (Figure 2.8) offers students verbs to self-reference their current understanding and next steps they need to take to progress.

Figure 2.6 **Stonefields Activation Images**

Stonefields School Learner Qualities	Stonefields Graphic Organizer	Play Structure With Learner Qualities

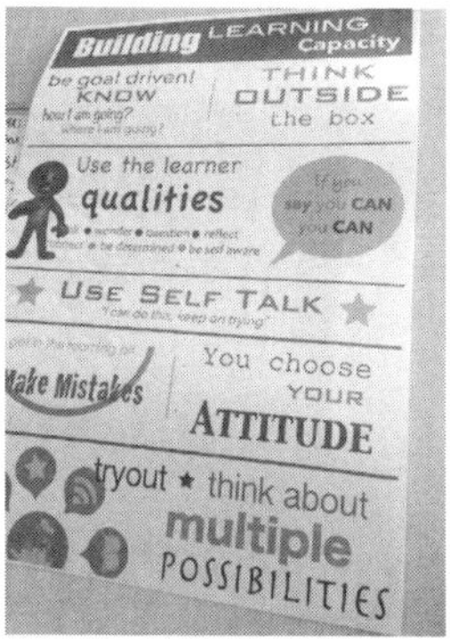

Source: Stonefields School, Auckland, New Zealand. Used with Permission.

Figure 2.7   Characteristics of "Visible Learners"

Source: Photo courtesy of LaTyia Rolle. Elk Grove, CA. Used with Permission.

Figure 2.8   *Where am I in my learning?* Poster

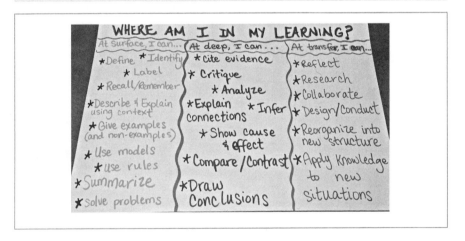

Source: Ross School; Ross, CA. Used with Permission.

Figure 2.9 provides a series of questions that teachers may use to identify a student's activation toward monitoring, evaluating, and improving their own learning.

Figure 2.9 Key Questions to Assess Students' Activation

Activation Criteria	Key Questions
Learning Dispositions	• What enables learners to persevere?
	• How do I learn?
	• What enables learners to recognize their successes and challenges?
	• What helps learners stay focused?
	• What strategies do I use when I'm bored?
	• What strategies have supported me in the past to learn content at surface, deep, and transfer?
	• What strategies do I use when I disagree? When I feel indifferent?
Learning Strategies	• What strategies do I use when I'm lost? What strategies do I use when I'm stuck?
	• What do I do when I don't know what to do?
	• What strategies do I use when I'm first learning something (surface)?
	• What strategies do I use when I'm proficient (deep)?
	• What strategies do I use to go beyond or to apply my learning (transfer)

Activation in the High School Context

Jen Mall, English Teacher
Sir Francis Drake High School
San Anselmo, California

In a high school setting, the most important element to a classroom that promotes learning over grades is to establish a deep trust between teacher

(Continued)

(Continued)

and students. Students are used to "gaming the system" and they see teachers as obstacles to their success rather than allies in their learning. So often students will ask my co-teacher and I in disbelief: "So if I don't do well the first time, I can try again?" When they first enter our classroom, they are wondering what the catch is.

In order to create a classroom like this, it's important to have a few big pieces in place before the school year even begins. When possible, I map out our entire semester's (or year if possible) learning goals and success criteria. I think about where I want my students to be at the end of the spring semester and map backward from there. Since high school students have a high stakes transcript grade that comes mid-year, I establish clear skill and content goals for fall and spring semester. The spring semester's goals are naturally more difficult than the fall semester's goals. Each of these goals have scoring scales that reflect what students will need to know and be able to do to be successful in that skill and/or content area. It's important to break the scales down for the students and scaffold opportunities for each student to reach proficiency (or get as close as possible) by the end of the semester.

I have found one of the most rewarding parts of structuring my classroom like this is that it allows for the most reluctant learner to begin to believe in him/herself again. Too often, incoming 9th graders have already established themselves as "terrible writers" or "terrible readers," and by giving them time and the opportunity to find success and make small steps toward improvement, they begin to think of themselves as readers and writers again, or in some cases, for the first time. The same is true for the highly anxious achievers who often avoid failing at all costs. By having the space to make mistakes without high stakes attached, these students take risks that they would have otherwise avoided in more traditional classroom settings, as often taking risks can prove costly to a student in today's high school classrooms.

The two biggest challenges I have found in this work are

1. Finding the right balance between giving students enough time to learn yet also having students meet important deadlines on time

2. Creating enough time for myself to give fast and effective feedback

Creating clear outcomes and allowing students to track their own learning are some of the ways to address both of these. Always a work in progress.

Collaboration

Collaboration is defined as the ability of students to work with others to give and receive feedback, co-construct ideas and solutions, and strengthen relationships with and among others. Learning is a social experience, and a student's ability to orient their learning, maintain an active engagement with learning, and develop expertise is inextricably linked to the power of working with, supporting, and learning from peers and teachers (McDowell, 2017). Figure 2.10 illustrates a series of questions that get to the core of social learning. These questions are seeking information regarding how well learners recognize and apply the tremendous power of the social aspect of learning and the need and desire to enhance each other's learning through shared understanding, debate, and collective action.

Figure 2.10   Key Questions (The 4Ps) to Assess Student Collaboration

Collaboration Criteria	Key Questions
Push	• How can others push my thinking? • What feedback can I seek to improve my learning? • How can others strengthen or challenge my ideas? • How do I push someone's thinking forward without telling them what I want them to do?
Pull	• How do I support others in pulling their thinking forward? • How do I pull someone's learning forward?
Press	• How do we collectively press forward and co-construct new ideas and solutions? • How do we celebrate and challenge our individual ideas to create a better solution together? • How do we press upon potential misconceptions, explore paradoxes, and understand the strengths and limitations of models (such as metaphors)?
Pause	• How do we pause our own ideas and listen to those from others? • How do we pause on our first response and think deeply about supporting others? • How do we "stay soft on people and hard on content"?

Activities 2.1, 2.2, and 2.3 are designed to enhance both student and teacher collaboration. The activities include: Checking our Stories, Establishing Agreements, and Creating Interactive Roles for Responsibility.

ACTIVITY 2.1
CHECKING OUR STORIES

There are often pervasive and powerful stories in schools that position students and teachers in an untenable position for developing, managing, and sustaining collaboration. Beyond the normal challenges of groups, teams, or basic interactions, there are a number of pernicious myths that prevent student teams in school from being highly effective. Below are several "myths" or stories that drive how people make decisions related to collaboration between and among students and adults.

Step 1: Review each myth.

Step 2: As a team (students and/or teachers), discuss the following questions:

1. Does this myth exist in our school, our classroom/department, and our team?
2. If so, how does this impact our ability to collaborate?
3. What next steps should we take to improve or enhance our learning?

Step 3: As a team, identify other myths that may be operating in the school, classroom/department, or team.

Myth 1: *We should treat students like experts.*

First, students are not experts in the field in which they are trying to problem solve with others: They are for the most part novices. Novices and experts think completely differently from one another in navigating how to solve a problem (Willingham, 2010). As discussed earlier, there is a difference between respecting students as human beings and expecting them to engage in work as experts engage in work. Often students do not have the foundational knowledge required in core content and in 21st Century skills, such as leading or participating in teams. This must be directly taught by teachers and continually assessed, with targeted feedback that students will use to move their learning forward. This logic should be applied equally to teams. Student teams are not expert teams.

Myth 2: *We should put kids in teams for everything.*

Teams are typically not required for each level of complexity (i.e., surface, deep, and transfer). Specifically, teams are not needed when individual students are developing surface and even deep level knowledge and skills. When students are put in teams at earlier stages, they often fail to discuss and debate central principles of academic disciplines, solve ill-defined problems, or evaluate proposed solutions because they lack academic knowledge and skill. This often leads to teams of students coming together to "divide and conquer" tasks that could be done by individual students and/or create presentations that lack meaningful insight into a novel problem. In essence, you get the "whomp a mole" syndrome where individual students pop up and present their set slide with no connection of message to other members' statements or the overall solution. When prompted to clarify, all students lack the ability to address the questions because they simply developed an efficient slide deck to present so they could be finished.

This is not to say that students should not collaborate. In fact, providing students with peer-to-peer feedback that is accurate will have a high likelihood of enhancing student learning (Wiliam, 2011). Moreover, this type of collaboration is great practice for when students are in teams at later stages of learning. Teams are a much bigger undertaking, and teachers should think about when they would maximize learning.

Myth 3: *Team structures drive team performance.*

In my early training and countless professional learning experiences on team dynamics, I continued to receive the following messages from presenters:

- Student teams should be comprised of four students.

- Spend your time identifying the composition of your team, which includes academic ability and emotional compatibility with others.

- Provide tools, such as rubrics and group contracts, to guide students as they work together.

The structure of teams is dependent on the team's purpose and function. Teams are valuable when they are used to

- Ensure students are progressing toward meeting transfer-level content and skill demands by addressing a challenging task

- Developing collaborative knowledge and skills to engage in team environments that address challenging tasks

Myth 4: *Teams are more effective when we minimize conflict.*

From a team perspective, conflict is a normal and essential attribute of groups (Karp, 1980). Albion and Gibson (2000) remarked that group problem-solving requires cognitive dissonance, which arises through discussion to challenge and reconsider individual and collective thinking around beliefs, assumptions, and prior knowledge. Unfortunately, adult teams in problem-solving situations face issues of identifying, testing, and intervening when inadequate reasoning, negotiation, and reflection are present. Moreover, teams have a difficult time discerning an idea from the person presenting the idea, and often teams defer decisions to an individual or minority opinion with minimal persuasion, critical debate, or reflection (Ochoa & Robinson, 2005).

The key strategy to focus on to ensure functional teams and effective group decisions is to allow for dissent and to encourage well thought-out arguments and substantiated debate. Teachers may have a tendency to keep their opinions to themselves (Schwarz, 2013) or not want to rock the boat—to go with the flow—but keeping our well-reasoned objections or ideas to ourselves will not result in the best outcomes for our students. Offering up a conflicting idea or argument is often the most important step to reaching an efficacious decision. Challenging prior misconceptions or biases is often a necessary strategy in developing better collective solutions that incorporate multiple perspectives, experiences, and shared learning. As Hargreaves, Boyle, and Harris (2014) stated, "Conflict is the lifeblood of creativity."

Myth 5: *Teams are a static structure.*

Teams are dynamic and constantly progressing or regressing in their development. O'Brien (1994) argued that team development is akin to the stages of human development. During the initial stages of life, team members are attempting to understand the purpose of the team and understand others and their own role. Tuckman and Jensen (1977) argue that this is the forming stage of a team's life. As an adolescent is struggling with finding a unique identity and conforming with others, teams are struggling to reconcile individual differences and collective similarities. Tuckman and Jensen (1977) refer to this stage as "storming," as the team is both clarifying their purpose as a team and addressing inherent conflicts amongst members. As discussed in Myth 4, this is an essential part of team life. As an individual matures into adulthood and begins to establish priorities and goals, the team begins to form a cohesive structure (i.e., norming) and, over time, develops proficiency, even mastery in their work (performing). All things, including those that are likely metaphors for living things, end (i.e., adjourning).

Like parents, each stage requires our awareness and strategies for supporting teams as they go through and transition beyond each stage.

Myth 6: *Focus on dividing tasks up between individuals rather than building relationships to engage in collaborative problem-solving.*

Teams require balancing both the relationships between and among team members, the emotional wellbeing of each team member, and the specific individual and team tasks at hand. Relationships are essential, but we should not put people into teams if the task doesn't require that level of collaboration.

Myth 7: *Teams are more creative than individuals.*

Teams are far better at iteration and converging to novel solutions, but they are not necessarily more generative, divergent, or better at yielding new discoveries than individuals. For example, extensive research on brainstorming illustrates that individuals generate far more ideas and much more novel ideas than people in group situations (Chamorro-Premuzic, 2015). Moreover, teams can be beset by power struggles, groupthink, and toxic relational challenges that can prevent people from generating new ideas. Yes, teams can be more creative over time than individuals, but giving individuals time to initially think about problems, wrestle with ideas, and have time throughout the team process to reflect on their own thinking makes for a much more powerful team experience and more effective solution.

Myth 8: *Teachers are team facilitators.*

There is some truth laden in each myth. Teams are often assisted in enhancing their performance by facilitators. The key differentiator on the efficacy of the facilitator comes down to their focus. The etymology of facilitate is important to keep in mind when working with and managing teams. The word *facilitate* means to "make easy, render less difficult, from French "*faciliter acilis "to render easy" from stem of Latin* "easy to do," *facere "to do" (from IE root *dhe-"to set put")* Facilitated; facilitates; facilitating* (facilitate, n.d.).

The trouble is that often, facilitators focus on the structural aspects of how teams work together (e.g., the best way to group students) rather than how teams work together to solve problems. Moreover, teams have this same view considering facilitators as "resource persons." That is, they look to teachers as those who will organize materials needed and provide the team rules and responsibilities for completing tasks. Through all of this, the facilitator is quite passive in engaging with teams in in solving challenging problems. Teachers would be far better suited to take a much more involved role in engaging with teams in their work. For examples, teachers should consider co-constructing conversation agreements and protocols with teams so that teams may develop a collective understanding of problems, identify potential solutions, select a solution, and implement solutions to problems.

Often this is based on teachers intervening when students have academic misunderstandings, interpersonal conflicts, and when exploring and testing assumptions and inferences.

Myth 9: *Teams perform gradually.*

Teams perform in bursts, not through incremental steps. Often teams confer, debate, plan, get stuck, and then show rapid progress. We like to think that learning looks like a linear process, but fits and starts are how people and groups of people actually learn and progress toward deadlines.

ACTIVITY 2.2
ESTABLISHING AGREEMENTS

In this activity, collaborative groups discuss agreements (or norms) that enhance their ability to interact via dialogue.

Step 1: Have the group create norms/agreements that the group should adhere to in a collaborative setting.

Step 2: Pose the following questions to the group/team:

1. *Do the following agreements/norms ensure that we are checking each other's thinking?*
2. *Do the following agreements/norms ensure that we are listening to each other's thinking?*
3. *Do the following agreements/norms enhance our ability to engage in dialogue and make a decision?*

Step 3: Have the group compare the Mighty 9 agreements listed below Step 4 to the agreements just created. Ask the group to address the following questions:

1. How do these agreements/norms compare to our own?
2. What changes if any should we make to our agreements/norms?

Step 4: Implement agreements.

The Mighty 9 Agreements
1. Create an agreed upon decision-making process.
2. Use that process to check for disagreements and to discuss "undiscussables."

The Mighty 9 Agreements
3. Use questions to address potential conflicts and to explore ideas.
4. Always check in on each member of the group to make sure they understand group process.
5. Each group member will explain their actions or beliefs to the group.
6. Each group member is responsible for all other group members in understanding the task and coaching each other to perform at a high level.
7. Each group member will explain important words and provide specific examples when needed.
8. All group members will question other members when they encounter "jump to conclusion" comments.
9. When sharing ideas, all members will advocate their ideas and ask questions about other ideas.

The key to team roles is to stimulate and maintain interaction between and among team members. One way of ensuring quality interactions between team members is by designing key roles that promote interaction. Typically, student roles have been based on increasing efficiency of tasks by dividing tasks up or breaking up specific processes to get tasks done faster (think about the assembly line). These roles amount to designing efficiency usually include (recorder, project manager, project designer, researcher).

As a teacher, I have watched students present a solution to a problem by taking turns sharing their contributions to the work. This approach belied a lack of unity or collective decision-making in determining a solution. Moreover students rarely talked to each other except to get assignments done. They did not participate in collective discussions aimed at determining a solution. This "divide and conquer" approach runs counter to ensuring students are learning and tackling transfer-level tasks. In fact, if the roles that are needed for a team involve "divide and conquer" approaches, then you don't need a team in the first place.

ACTIVITY 2.3
CREATING INTERACTIVE ROLES FOR RESPONSIBILITY

In this activity, participants explore the importance of roles to stimulate dialogue and debate. Next, participants create roles that meet such interactive expectations.
Participants: students or teachers

Step 1: (2–3 minutes) Ask participants to discuss the importance of individual roles and responsibilities to

- Improve group and team dynamics (relationships)
- Create a collaborative solution

Step 2: Ask participants to identify specific roles and responsibilities that enhance how a group works.

Step 3: Propose the following goal for the group:

Groups are specifically designed to engage in dialogue and debate to solve transfer-level tasks.

Step 4: Ask the group to review their roles and determine if the roles and responsibilities they created will fulfill the proposed goal.

Step 5: Have the group review the proposed roles to (a) compare and contrast the proposed roles to those developed and (b) potentially implement the roles in their groups.

The following roles are suggested as a way to catalyze team dialogue . . .

Examples of Group Roles	
Process Observer	The purpose of this role is to ensure that agreements (e.g., The Mighty 9 from Activity 2.2), protocols (e.g., Resource 6.1 Critical Friends), and roles are established and maintained during the duration the team is together.
	They often begin meetings and have group members review the agreements before the team engages in dialogue or completes tasks. The process observer will often reference protocols when the team is engaging in feedback. Furthermore, the process observer intervenes when agreements are violated and protocols are not adhered to when meeting.

Examples of Group Roles	
Precision Coach	The purpose of this role is to ensure the information people are collecting, sharing, and documenting is accurate and relevant (linked to the success criteria and the context of the transfer task) and that all members have a clear understanding of the task and background knowledge as well as the context. Summarizing and checking for understanding is an essential part of this role. The precision coach typically asks others to cite their sources, paraphrase what they have stated, and connect their statements to success criteria.
Perspective Coach	The purpose of this role is to ensure that the viewpoints of each team member are brought to the discussion and that viewpoints of others outside the group/team that are impacted by the decisions of the group/team are considered.
Primer	The purpose of this role is to promote convergent and divergent thinking. The primer will set times for teams to step back and review the entire task and generate questions to brainstorm potential solutions or move the group toward convergent thinking.

After having completed activities such as assessing myths, establishing group norms, and creating roles that promote interaction, use the following questions in Figures 2.4, 2.9, and 2.10 to collect evidence regarding your students' efficacy. Based on the data collected, assess your students' level of efficacy in your class via Figure 2.11. Figure 2.11 offers suggested behaviors that emerge when first learning efficacious strategies (Introducing Efficacy), when developing competency (Applying Efficacious Behaviors), and when fully established (Reinforcing Efficacious Behaviors). Once you determine whether your class or a student is at the introductory phase, the application phase, or the reinforcing phase then you can apply strategies to move a student to the next phase by applying visual learning resources, learning triads, and agreements/protocols (see Figure 2.12).

Figure 2.11 Progression of Developing Efficacious Behaviors

	Orientation	Activation	Collaboration
Introducing Efficacy Teachers are spending significant time providing background information on the need for efficacious behaviors and are trying different strategies that they may use consistently in the future. Students are often unclear of the terminology, routines, and strategies that are being used in the classroom.	• Learners are unclear on the goals of learning, the expectations of meeting goals, and next steps related to improving their learning. • Learners are unclear on levels of learning and how to talk about developing their learning across levels of complexity. • Learner reflections are often focused on task performance and meeting task deadlines.	• Learners are unclear on strategies that would support them in learning when they are stuck, bored, or indifferent. • Learners are uncomfortable discussing their performance and "feel bad" when they fail. • Learners often associate the best learners as those who get As, answer questions immediately and correctly, and are compliant.	• Learners are inconsistent or inaccurate with giving and receiving feedback that aligns with success criteria. • Learners are uncomfortable sharing their work and receiving feedback. • Learners often disengage in dialogue when solving collective problems where opinions vary.
Applying Efficacious Behaviors Routines are emerging in classrooms and are conducted largely by teachers, with several gentle reminders throughout the day. Students are often being redirected to structure their individual and collective work using efficacious strategies.	• Learners understand the learning intentions and the success criteria of meeting intentions but lack a plan for improving their learning. • Learners have a clear sense of their proficiency and growth in meeting learning goals while failing to relate such learning to levels of complexity.	• Learners have attempted strategies that would support them in learning when they are stuck, bored, or indifferent. • Learners are comfortable discussing their performance and have an openness to discussing their work in public.	• When prompted and scaffolded, learners are giving and receiving accurate feedback related to success criteria and exemplars. • Learners state they are comfortable in giving and receiving feedback. • When prompted and scaffolded, learners engage in dialogue to solve problems.

	Orientation	Activation	Collaboration
	• Learners continue to struggle with the relationship between classroom activities, contexts, and the success criteria.	• Learners often associate the best learners as those who are making changes to improve their own learning.	
Reinforcing Efficacious Behaviors Routines are in place that are conducted largely by students without reminders from adults. Students are often reinforcing a focus on learning through the way they structure their individual and collective work.	• Learners are measuring their own proficiency and progress toward surface, deep, and transfer expectations and plotting out next steps to improve. • Learners are questioning their prior knowledge and reflecting on steps they can take to improve upon their current understanding. • Learners clearly articulate the relationship between classroom activities, contexts, and the success criteria.	• Learners are utilizing strategies that enable themselves to persevere when they are bored, stuck, or indifferent about the work. • Learners are reflecting and planning for how to transfer such skills to other parts of their life.	• Learners are giving and receiving accurate feedback to others. • Learners are solving complex problems by integrating the ideas of others and testing assumptions. • Learners use agreements, protocols, and norms to maintain relationships and solve problems.

Leading the Development of Student Efficacy

Lexie Cala, Principal
Bel Aire Elementary School
Tiburon, California

I am relatively new to this work, but its impact on my leadership has been powerful and profound. I am blessed with a talented teaching staff, and learning has always been visible throughout our school, but we lacked coherence and a clear, shared focus. Engaging in this work affirmed some of our existing practices, but with practical guidance, we have established a renewed clarity and passion for what we do. In short, we are refining our *individual* and *collective efficacy.*

Our biggest shift is simple: a singular focus on learning. Simple is not easy however, and maintaining this focus has necessitated we are just as thoughtful about what we choose to do as we are about what we choose not to do. Change has intentionally been implemented slowly but deliberately and with observable impact.

Our progress and process is rooted in Orientation, Activation, and Collaboration (O.A.C.). As part of our *Orientation* work, we clarified our focus around learning progressions and processes. We asked ourselves the three essential questions (Where are we? Where are we going? and How will we get there?). We examined research-supported learning influences and high-impact learning strategies, and we continually evaluate our work against its impact on student learning. Equally important, we continue to let go of those tempting shiny objects that are new, popular, familiar, distracting, or easy but unlikely to move the learning dial.

We initially landed on a small, focused commitment to improve our learners' ability to be self-regulated, or *assessment capable.* Specifically, students are asked to answer the same three essential questions (Where am I in my learning? Where am I going? and How will I get there?). We quickly realized that developing assessment-capable learners required us to do the following: better articulate learning intentions, clarify success criteria, improve the quality of our feedback, and hold regular conversations about what it means to be a good learner.

As part of our implementation, or *Activation* work, we continue to support a schoolwide culture that embraces growth, risk-taking, and challenge. We clarify and model those beliefs and behaviors that will enhance learning rather than only those that ensure compliant behavior. We emphasize how we behave during a challenge and what to do when we don't know what to do. And we are careful to revisit these beliefs and behaviors when it is most impactful and relevant, which is during those moments a learner is stuck or in the Learning Pit.

Both young and adult learners select achievable targets and learning strategies for the greatest impact. Ongoing feedback informs our next steps, and we use assessment as a means to *improve* rather than simply to *measure* learning. Our next step is to more explicitly align and articulate tasks, strategies, and assessment to surface, deep, and transfer-levels of learning.

The entirety of this work is deeply rooted in *Collaboration*. One of the reasons this work has been so impactful is because we are all (young and adult learners) following the same trajectory and charting our progress in this iterative O.A.C. process. The tasks may differ, but we are all answering the same *three essential questions*, practicing effective *learner dispositions*, and giving and receiving *feedback*. There is great power in this shared work as a means to not only bolster learning but also to build culture.

We acknowledge that we are at different points in our learning, and we openly share our successes and our challenges. Learners are talking more about their strategies to improve their own learning and that of others. Teachers model instructional strategies during staff meetings so that adults can similarly improve their own practice and that of others. Each classroom hosts a weekly schoolwide meeting where we highlight a learning strategy or learner disposition. As the leader, I attempt to reinforce our learning and our focus via articles, links, and other resources in my weekly written communication with staff. In addition to learning with each other, I promote outside professional development only when it is precisely aligned with our work and our narrow focus. And I participate with my teachers in these PD opportunities because it is my responsibility to model collaborative learning.

In developing individual and collective efficacy, we are chipping away at one of the largest barriers to learning: within school variability. As a leader, my primary role is to harness the expertise of my highly qualified teachers and to inspire them to continually reinvest in their practice by sharing my own passion for this work, building positive relationships, and maintaining an unrelenting focus on learning.

Again, that is the big and simple picture: a *focus on learning*. Fidelity to this focus requires ongoing and purposeful adjustments. Specifically, I guide conversations toward the influences that matter and away from the "politics of distraction." I promote a climate that focuses on risk-taking and growth, not one of compliance. I have redesigned my process for hiring teachers to

(Continued)

(Continued)

include questions aimed to unmask beliefs about learning. Perhaps one of the most significant shifts I have made has been my own mindset around formal evaluations (which generally have a pretty low effect size). I can finally see this process as a genuine opportunity to support teacher growth by sharing my success criteria and limiting feedback to only that which is aligned with our focus. I have found this simple shift has resulted in more meaningful conversations and improved teacher practice, and I can now use what was once a stressful yet low-impact process to punctuate the ongoing importance of our focus on learning.

Although a focus on learning seems obvious and "simple," it has been shocking to see how frequently the politics of distraction thwart this effort with seemingly urgent and important conversations. One of the reasons we have found this work to be so appealing and accessible is because of its clarity and simplicity. McDowell says, "*It is that simple—and that hard*," and it is so true! It's simplicity lies in the clarity, but such an unrelenting focus on learning requires great effort. This effort however, has real impact for our learners. Seeing evidence of our impact is one of the most powerful ways to help us reinvest in our important work and thereby move us forward on our journey toward improved individual and collective efficacy.

Teaching Strategies for Developing Student Efficacy

There are a number of strategies that may be implemented in the classroom to cultivate efficacy (i.e., orientation [O], activation [A], and collaboration [C]. In this chapter we look at incorporating visual resources, learning triad routines, agreements, and protocols into teacher and learner classroom practice (see Figure 2.12). Visual resources may be defined as a scaffold that may be used as a reference for key information and as a means to track data. Learning triads are a collaborative-based approach to reflect on learning, give and receive feedback, and solve challenging transfer-level problems. Agreements and protocols are strategies for structuring conversations and solving problems (see Figure 2.27 and 2.29).

Figure 2.12 **Efficacy-Based Strategies Overview**

Strategies	Visual Resources	Learning Triad Routines	Agreements and Protocols
Orientation	• Progress and Proficiency Matrix (Resource 6.13b) • Depth of Complexity Discussion Scaffold (Resource 6.13d) • Progress Reference Cues (Figures 2.15–2.18)	• Learning Zone Discussion • Bags are packed	• Agreements • Share all relevant information • Use specific examples • Protocols • Constructivist Listening (Resource 6.7) • SWOT Analysis Protocol (Resource 6.3)
Activation	• The Learning Pit • Feedback • Feedback Thinking Prompts • Visual Cue Success Frame	• Bookend meetings • Choose your own strategy	• Agreements • Test assumptions and inferences • Protocol • Gap Analysis Protocol (Resource 6.4)
Collaboration	• Inquiry Prompt Charts	• Inspect performance and identify next steps in learning • Focus and Flare	• Agreements • Explain reasoning and intent • Share views and ask genuine questions • Protocols (Resources 6.1, 6.2, 6.6) • Critical Friends • What? So What? Now What? • Learning Dilemma

Visual Resources

In schools that have developed efficacious learners, there are number of visual cues that include images, processes, and bulleted lists of criteria that allow learners to think about, discuss, and take action on their learning. When these resources are displayed in a classroom with images and text that students can understand or created by students themselves, they assist in the creation of a culture of learning. When routinely utilized by students, there is a higher likelihood that they will develop efficacy.

Classroom teachers may use a myriad of strategies to enable students to have a clear sense of the learning intentions of the unit or lesson, their current progress, and the next steps they are going to take to improve. (See Figures 2.13–2.17: Progress and Proficiency Charts, Depth of Complexity Charts, and Progress Reference Cues.)

In Figure 2.13, a kindergartener is in the process of writing his first ever personal narrative. This photo shows him comparing his work to success criteria and successful examples (or models of work) at each level of complexity (i.e., surface, deep, and transfer).

When Teddy began his personal narrative, he knew that he had mastered the surface level criteria because he could compare his work to that of the visual models displayed in the classroom. He was able to revise drafts of his work over time and recognize how his work had improved based on the success criteria. Having now written his personal narrative and compared it to the transfer model displayed in the class, he is attempting to identify what steps he needs to take to move from deep learning to transfer learning. To view Video 2.1 "Draft of Teddy's Work," use your smartphone to click on the QR code or visit the companion website at http://resources.corwin.com/DevelopingExpertLearners.

Video 2.1 Draft of Teddy's Work

http://resources
.corwin.com/
DevelopingExpert
Learners

Progress and Proficiency Charts

Our kindergarten learner could use both the visual orientation resource seen in Figure 2.13 and the Progress and Proficiency matrix (Figure 2.1) to reflect on his progress over time. Having written his personal narrative and seeing his growth from surface to deep, he would now likely consider his learning to be high growth and high performance (high proficiency) because he knows what high proficiency looks like and he can recognize the improvements shown in his current work as compared to his work earlier in the school year. This is one example of a student developing expertise not only in writing but in developing his efficacy by

Figure 2.13   **Student Assessment of Work via Leveled Success Criteria**

Source: Ross School; Ross, CA. Used with permission.

evaluating his own work—and note that this can be done quite well at the kindergarten level.

Depth of Complexity Charts

One way to support students in understanding the levels of complexity in learning is to use metaphors.

Figure 2.14 illustrates one metaphor that has been found to be helpful to learners. Figure 2.14 uses a snorkeler, scuba diver, and the astronaut to represent surface, deep, and transfer respectively. In my own experience, metaphors have been a powerful way for students to conceptualize a rather abstract idea. In their 2017 book, Almarode and Miller utilized the metaphor of the snorkeler and the scuba diver to symbolize the ideas of being a learner at the surface and deep levels of learning (Almarode and Miller did not use the astronaut as part of the metaphor for transfer). The snorkel is at the surface of the ocean observing the ecosystems below. The snorkeler is unable to explore the depths of the ocean, much like the learner who is unable to connect ideas together; essentially, both can only survey the scene. The scuba diver symbolizes someone who is at a much deeper level of learning. The scuba diver has transitioned from being at the surface of the ocean to being able to explore the depths of the ocean. She has a deeper sense of the ocean, much like the learner who has a deeper sense of the content and skills she is exploring. In another metaphor altogether, the astronaut symbolizes the ability to apply the concepts of gravity and oxygen in different environments. An example of the Depth of Complexity Cues is shown in Figure 2.13. If you look closely, you can see that Teddy is looking at an image of a snorkeler under the Surface column, an image of the scuba diver under the Deep column, and an astronaut under the Transfer column. Figure 2.14 illustrates how teachers could visually represent depth of complexity with success criteria.

Figure 2.14   Complexity Metaphor for Students

Depth of Complexity	Description	Strategies That Support Me at This Level	Next Steps: To Go Deeper I Will . . .
	SURFACE I can understands ideas and/or skills.	• Outlining • Mnemonics • Summarization • Note-taking • Rehearsal	I will connect those ideas by . . .
	DEEP I can relate ideas and/or skills	• Seeking help from peers • Classroom discussions • Evaluations and reflections	I will apply these ideas by . . .

Depth of Complexity	Description	Strategies That Support Me at This Level	Next Steps: To Go Deeper I Will . . .
	TRANSFER I can apply ideas/and or skills in different situations.	• Seeing patterns in new situations • Identifying similarities and differences in problems	I will seek to apply these ideas in the future by . . .

Source: leremy/iStock.com

Progress Reference Cues

Progress reference cues are visual displays in the classroom that students use to represent their progress and proficiency during class instruction. Students may use cues such as Figure 2.15 and Figure 2.16 to determine and elicit their understanding as they enter a new day in class, tackle a new task, engage in a discussion, or perhaps, receive feedback. Figure 2.15 frames for students three categories for when they are discussing their learning. The Comfort Zone refers to students that find the situation easy, possibly boring, and redundant. The Learning Zone refers to students who are struggling to understand but have enough support that they are able to follow along assimilating new information, ask questions, seek and use feedback, and actively engage with new material or new tasks. The Panic Zone refers to a state of feeling overwhelmed and not understanding the expectations, the new content, or new skills. Students have used the following Learning Zone cues to discuss with others where they believe they are in their learning and what steps they need to take to be in the Learning Zone. This is, of course, one of many options. Some teachers have used physical identifiers on desks including cups that students may show to

Figure 2.15   The Learning Zone Cue

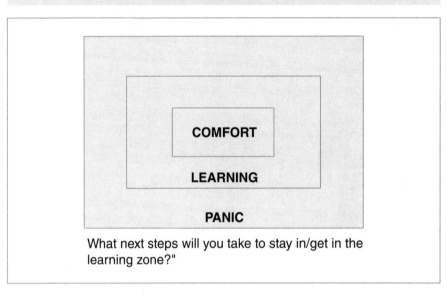

What next steps will you take to stay in/get in the learning zone?"

Source: Ross School in Ross, CA. Used with permission.

the teacher (see Figure 1.5). Other teachers have embedded the zones of learning on assignments for students to reference (see Figure 2.16).

Cues such as Figure 2.17 enable students to see successful levels of performance (1—Beginning, 2—Approaching, 3—Proficiency, and 4—Advanced) as well as success criteria for each level of performance and examples at each level. This enables students to self-reference and work with peers to identify where they are in their learning, where they need to go, and craft next steps.

Activation Strategies
(The Learning Pit, Feedback
Thinking Prompts, Visual Cue Success Frame)

Providing learners with visual references to remind them of what makes (and what it takes to be) a strong learner, strategies that will support learners in their learning, and reminders of how to persevere when they get stuck, bored, or don't care about the subject has been found in the field to make a substantial impact on student efficacy over time. The Learning Pit, Feedback Thinking Prompts, and Success Learner posters are a few visual references that have a high likelihood of supporting learner activation.

Figure 2.16   Learning Zone Self-Reflection

Student Name:

| My Learning Goal: | I am working on an Informative "How To" Writing project |
| | *(I can draw or write to help me share what I think)* |

⊙ I can choose my "How To" writing topic
(CCSS.ELA-LITERACY.W.K.2)

⊙ I can draw pictures and number my steps on a graphic organizer
(CCSS.ELA-LITERACY.W.K.2)

⊙ I can label important parts of my pictures
(CCSS.ELA-LITERACY.W.K.2)

⊙ I can include clear directions and sequence words (first, second, next, last)
(CCSS.ELA-LITERACY.W.K.2)

⊙ I can create a cover and assemble my finished book
(CCSS.ELA-LITERACY.W.K.2)

Date 2-6-18

What is your "How To" topic?

Teaching a baby colors,

Date 3-1-18

Now I am able to (Where am I now?) come up with my "how to"
steps.

I am still working on (Where am I going?) getting the right
words on the right page.

My next steps are (How do we get there?) use pictures to
help me choose my words.

Figure 2.17   Progression Levels Poster

Source: Photo courtesy of LaTyia Rolle. Elk Grove, CA. Used with Permission.

The Learning Pit

One of the key elements of supporting students in developing in the area of activation is to provide them strategies that enhance their performance and emotional responses when facing challenges. One of the most practical and powerful ways to frame this idea with students is to use James Nottingham's (2017b) *The Learning Challenge*. The idea behind the learning pit is that, when students learn new material, they must encounter challenges to what they previously thought, often engaging in cognitive conflict. With support (e.g., attempting new strategies, feedback, deliberate practice, etc.), they eventually emerge from the pit, developing new ideas and skills. Every successful learner goes through the learning pit. Once they are out of the pit, they celebrate, reflect, and then they go back in, starting the process again. Figure 2.18 shows a version of the learning pit found in James Nottingham's (2017) book, *The Learning Challenge*.

Feedback Thinking Prompts

Research continues to show that when feedback is utilized to improve student performance, the rate of learning doubles. Moreover, as discussed, the majority of the feedback students get is from their peers and it is incorrect. Over the past five years, I have found that students more readily and accurately give and receive feedback when they have prompts and cues to support their emotions when encountering feedback. Figure 2.19 illustrates a series of prompts as well as the idea of grit being a key factor for students to handle feedback.

Figure 2.20 provides a frame for students to focus on the expectations of their learning, their current performance, and what next steps they need to take to improve their learning. This level of clarity is essential for students to reference where they may need feedback and support as they learn. Moreover, this example illustrates certain goals that require supporting others in their learning, which is a reinforcement of the importance of feedback.

Figure 2.21 illustrates characteristics (or dispositions or powers) that students use when they are "in the pit." Imagine a student who is stuck referencing this poster for a moment of self-reflection before going to the teacher for help. Wouldn't that student feel

Figure 2.18   The Learning Challenge

The Main Steps in the Learning Challenge

Easy Learning

Deep Learning

Concept
Find a concept worth exploring that you know a little bit about.

Question
Find the problems, the nuances, and the exceptions to your concept. You can do this by comparing your concept with another, considering if it always applies, or trying to find a definition that works in all cases.

The Pit

Cognitive Conflict
If you've uncovered lots of examples and exceptions to your concept, and realized how complex your chosen concept is, then you are in The Pit! This is where deep learning really gets going.

Construct
Identify patterns, relationships, and meanings between all the ideas you've uncovered. Distinguish between them by sorting, classifying, grouping, or ranking. Use your findings to create a more precise understanding of your concept.

Consider
Look back at your learning journey. Which strategies worked best? What would you change next time? How can you apply your new understanding to different contexts?

Eureka!
Eureka: you found it! The feeling of enlightenment and discovery you feel at this stage is the ecstasy of learning. This is what makes the learning journey so worthwhile. Congratulations for persevering!

Adapt

Apply

Transfer

Review

Challenging LEARNING

Source: Nottingham, James and Nottingham, Jill. *The Learning Challenge* (2017). Challenging Learning, Ltd. Used with permission.

more empowered if he were able to reflect on this own thinking himself rather than feeling that he needed the teacher to pull him out of the pit?

Collaboration (*Inquiry Prompt Charts*)

Visual references—such as inquiry prompting charts, agreements, and protocol posts—are means for supporting students in giving and receiving feedback between students that move learning forward. Additionally, these strategies are helpful to support students to solve complex tasks with others.

Figure 2.19   Feedback Cues Poster

Source: Gomez, J. (2018) Ross School; Ross, CA. Used with permission.

Figure 2.20   Visual Cue Success Frame

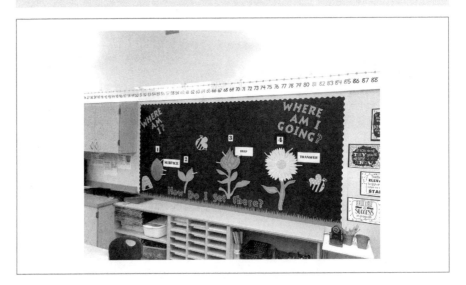

Source: Photo courtesy of Maggie Baker, Ross School District. Used with permission.

Figure 2.21   What Can I Say to Myself?

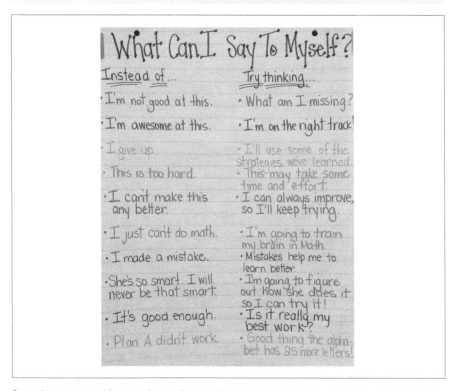

Source: Photo courtesy of Stephanie Skelton. Fieldcrest Elementary, Bradford, Ontario, Canada. Used with permission.

Inquiry Prompt Charts

An inquiry prompt chart helps learners direct their questions to themselves and others on how to continue to grow in their learning across levels of complexity (surface, deep, and transfer).

Learning Triad Routines

Beyond visual references, classroom teachers may want to consider embedding collaborative-based routines to support learners in consistently engaging with others in the areas of efficacy and expertise. Zbar (2013) recommend triads as the ideal group size to encourage challenging conversations while remaining small enough to maintain emotional safety. Figures 2.23, 2.24, and 2.25 illustrate a series of routines that are designed to develop students' capacity in the areas of orientation, activation, and collaboration.

   Pre- and Post-Assessment Progress Vignette: In the following high school classroom, students are tasked with reflecting on the progress and proficiency of students relative to pre- and post-assessment data across four class periods. The students then discuss what

Figure 2.22   Inquiry Prompt Chart

Surface	Deep	Transfer
• Does your/our answer meet the success criteria? • Is your/our answer correct/incorrect? • How can you/we elaborate on the answer? • What did you/we do well? • Where did you/we go wrong? • What is the correct answer?	• What is wrong and why? • What strategies did you/we use? • What is the explanation for the correct answer? • What other questions can you/we ask about the task? • What are the relationships with other parts of the task?	• How can you/we monitor your own work? • How can you/we carry out self-checking? • How can you/we evaluate the information provided? • How can you/we reflect on your own learning? • What might you/we do next time? • How could you improve this work? • What did you do to . . .? • How is this problem different from other problems? What is the same in the problem? • When and where does your/our strategy work? What other strategies may work?

Figure 2.23   Orientation Routines

	Learning Zone Discussion	Bags Are Packed
Description	• Students share their level of challenge with the daily lesson with others. 1. Comfort zone—green (refers to a student already having proficiency in that area) 2. Learning zone—yellow (refers to a student being challenged and able to manage the challenge)	• Students share their steps with the triad for meeting the learning intentions and success criteria of the unit. • After the presentations, members of the triad ask questions that ensure students have answered the three fundamental questions.

	Learning Zone Discussion	Bags Are Packed
	3. Panic zone—red zone (refers to a student being challenged and overwhelmed by the challenge they face) • Students work together to identify steps that will have a high probability of moving and keeping students in the learning zone.	
Steps	• Students meet in triads. • All students review the learning intentions and success criteria of the unit/lesson. • Students share their individual rating (green, yellow, red). • Each student shares their rationale for their rating. • Students work together to identify next steps to get into and stay in the yellow zone. • Students share their discussions and plan of action with the class.	• Students meet in triads. • All students review the learning intentions and success criteria of the unit/lesson. • Students share their plan individually. • Students share their discussions and plan of action with the class.
Variations	• Students may use visual displays such as colored cups, laminated pages with the learning zone targets, google sheets, etc.	• Hypotheticals—What if the plan doesn't work out? How will you handle setbacks that are unforeseen? • Use protocols to deepen the conversation (see Resource 6.6 Learning Dilemma Protocol). • Reflective meeting (How'd we do?).

Figure 2.24 Activation Routines

	Bookend Meetings	Choose Your Own Strategy
Description	• This routine enables learners to see their growth over a class period (or unit) in terms of their behaviors (and eventually beliefs).	• This routine enables learners to inspect the impact of strategies on their learning.
Steps	• Students identify beliefs (i.e., powers) and behaviors (i.e., strategies) they will use as they encounter challenges today. • Mid-lesson stop. • Students will reflect on their emotions and actions after the challenge they faced.	• Students identify a situation they are facing. • They generate a list of strategies that could be used. • They select one and identify how they will determine success or failure.
Variations	• Start with a fictitious profile of a learner and have students identify what this learner needs to do to get better in their learning.	• Students pair-share a fictitious profile of a learner and identify what this learner needs to do to get better in their learning.

Figure 2.25 Collaboration Routines

	Inspector	Focus and Flare
Description	• The following routine is designed to give and receive feedback as a means to move student performance to the next level.	• The following routine is designed to support groups in solving problems.
Steps	• Individual students share their progress and proficiency data with others. • Students then give and receive feedback related to the data. • These steps are related for every member of the triad. • Specific protocols are used with fidelity to give and receive feedback.	• **Focus**—students identify a potential problem that they are attempting to solve (this includes reviewing learning intentions and success criteria). • **Flare**—students individually brainstorm potential solutions. • **Focus**—students share their ideas and develop a solution to implement. The group develops a short-/long-term action plan.

	Inspector	Focus and Flare
Variations	• Students use the fishbowl method to engage in the discussion, focusing on one student throughout the meeting. • Students use a variety of protocols to evaluate their impact (e.g., Resource 6.1 Critical Friends Protocol, Resource 6.5 Constructivist Tuning Protocol).	• Reverse the focus and flare approach and reflect on the impact of the group's work and solutions devised. • Flare—receive feedback on solution implement and design/implementation of short-/long-term plan. • Focus—in light of feedback, the student makes adjustments to plan and reflects on next steps to improve.

strategies appeared to be helpful for the class to make substantial progress in their learning. The teacher writes a collective list for all classes to review and utilize during the next unit of instruction.

Agreements/Protocols

In addition to visual resources and collaboration routines, the classroom works effectively when agreements and protocols are established to focus the group on efficacy and expertise. Agreements are norms, rules, or colloquially "the way we work together" for how groups or teams function. For example, teachers may establish the following agreement: *Share all relevant information,* which requires learners to

- Disclose their prior knowledge, current thinking, and potential ideas to others

- Share inferences or assumptions that they believe are critical for the conversation

This agreement supports teachers and students in developing orientation-based skills for all learners by establishing up front the expectations of behavior.

Protocols are ways to structure conversations and problem-solving. One way to think of protocols is "how" people work together. Agreements are "what" the expectations are for working together. Let's take for example the agreement we reviewed earlier: *Share all relevant information.* One way to ensure that relevant information is shared is to use a protocol to elicit relevant information. There are

Figure 2.26   Pre- and Post-Assessments Visual

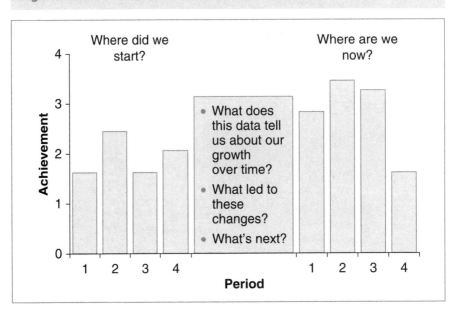

Source: Ross School; Ross, CA.

many protocols that can support students and teachers in giving and receiving feedback, including Resource 6.1 the Critical Friends Protocol, Resource 6.2 the What? So What? Now What? Protocol, and Resource 6.6 the Learning Dilemma Protocol. Figure 2.27 is a poster from the Ross School depicting one classroom's interpretation of how to implement the Critical Friends Protocol.

Figure 2.28 (Orientation Agreements and Protocols), Figure 2.29 (Activation Agreements and Protocols), and Figure 2.30 (Collaboration Agreements and Protocols) offer a sampling of agreements and protocols in the areas of orientation, activation, and collaboration respectively.

Conclusion

A culture is the result of people working together on recurring problems, in this case, improving academic and efficacy-based learning. The culture of developing expertise and efficacy is one that does the following:

1. Focuses on the problem of enhancing learning at surface, deep, and transfer and building efficacy (orientation, activation, and collaboration)

Figure 2.27   Critical Friends Process Poster

Source: Photo courtesy of Gomez, J. and Maxine Mannion. Used with permission.

Figure 2.28   Set I: Orientation Agreements and Protocols

Agreements	What does this mean?	What does it look like?	How do we seek opportunities to get better?
Share all relevant information.	• Learners are expected to disclose their prior knowledge, current thinking, and potential ideas to others.	• Scenario: Learners engage in a What? So What? Now What? Protocol (Resource 6.2). Learners focus on	• Teaching Learners: To support learners in sharing information provide prompts for students to

(Continued)

Figure 2.28   (Continued)

Agreements	What does this mean?	What does it look like?	How do we seek opportunities to get better?
	• Learners are expected to share inferences or assumptions that they believe is critical for the conversation.	the first two steps (What? and So What?) by asking questions, What else? Tell me more. What are we missing? to the group as they populate information.	use such as the following: ○ Thank you for sharing; can you tell me more? ○ If you presented the information differently, how would you do it?
Use specific examples.	• Learners are expected to define key terms to others and share examples through stories, metaphors, physical examples, images, etc.	• Scenario: Learners are asked to discuss key principles in a discipline. Learners are expected to share concrete examples for each principle to support overall learning of others.	• Teaching Learners: To support learners in using specific examples, teachers may provide prompts (What does this look like? What does it compare to? Have you seen this in a movie? Read this in a book? Have you experienced this in your life? How would you present this to a younger student?)

Figure 2.29   Set II: Activation Agreements and Protocols

Agreements	What does this mean?	What does it look like?	How do we seek opportunities to get better?
Test assumptions and inferences.	• Learners ask questions to explore facts that create	• Learners ask a series of clarifying questions and use paraphrasing to	• To teach learners how to test for assumptions and inferences, teachers

Agreements	What does this mean?	What does it look like?	How do we seek opportunities to get better?
Test assumptions and inferences.	inference and propose alternative ideas.	ensure they understand exactly what the presenter or text is presenting. • Learners engage in "exploring multiple stories" by asking what other perceptions, viewpoints are here?	steps should constantly present alternative viewpoints or perspectives to the most obvious assumption or inference. • Utilize a Tuning Protocol to explore ways to improve and identify next steps.

Figure 2.30	Set III: Collaboration Agreements and Protocols

Agreements	What does this mean?	What does it look like?	How do we seek opportunities to get better?
Explain reasoning and intent.	• The expectation is that when someone communicates they provide a clear rationale for their comments and the intent to which they are offering such content.	• When a learner speaks, they are prompted to provide a rationale for an opinion and their intent for sharing.	• Teaching learners to essentially back up what they say and expect the same from others while assuming and keeping positive intent. The best way to get better is to practice and give and receive feedback on explaining reasoning and intent.
Share views and ask genuine questions.	• The expectation is that learners need to	• When a learner communicates, they share their views and present a	• Teaching students to share views and ask genuine questions can be

(Continued)

Figure 2.30   (Continued)

Agreements	What does this mean?	What does it look like?	How do we seek opportunities to get better?
	balance advocacy of their view and inquiry into others' views.	question, expecting others to respond.	amplified by providing prompts for students to use when they communicate. E.g., I think _____. What do you think? We should _____. Do you see it differently? How are our ideas similar and different?

2. Collects evidence of student efficacy through a myriad of tools and questions

3. Takes action to improve efficacy and expertise by displaying and using visual resources, ensuring students engage in collaborative routines, and adhering to a set of agreements and protocols

In the next several chapters, we will look into the work required to build student expertise via teacher planning, teaching, and investing in collaboration with colleagues.

REFLECTION QUESTIONS

- What stands out for you in this chapter?
- How do you currently collect evidence of efficacy in your classrooms?
- What areas of efficacy (orientation, activation, and collaboration) do you think are opportunities for growth in your own practice and your students' practices?
- What are the recurring problems that you focus on in your classroom? How do your behaviors support such a focus?

- What strategies do you have in place right now to build student efficacy?

- What previous practices would you like to reinforce? What new practices would you like to implement?

ACTIVITIES

ACTIVITY 2.4
ORIENTATION ACTIVITY

Relationship Between Depth of Complexity and Success Criteria

One of the key aspects of building efficacy is to enable students to have a clear sense of the core expectations of learning across levels of complexity (surface, deep, and transfer).

Step 1: Find a small group of teachers and brainstorm a set of resources you could provide to students that would enable them to know specifically the

Figure 2.31 Surface, Deep, and Transfer Linking Visual Resource

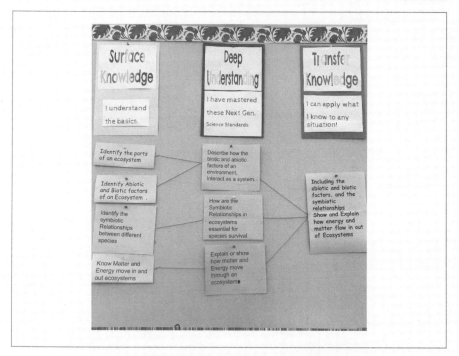

Source: J. Albertazzi, Silverado Middle School, Napa, CA (personal communication, 2018)

expectations of learning and how they would know their own performance over time (see Figure 2.17 for example).

Figure 2.31 shows the relationship between surface-level, deep-level, and transfer-level criteria. Learners wanted to visually display the relationship between different criteria and placed a shoestring between two or more criteria.

- -

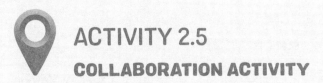

ACTIVITY 2.5

COLLABORATION ACTIVITY

Step 1: In each dotted box in Figure 2.32, have students draft prompts they can use when they are collaborating with their peers. (See Figure 2.33 for example.)

Figure 2.32   **4Ps Prompts**

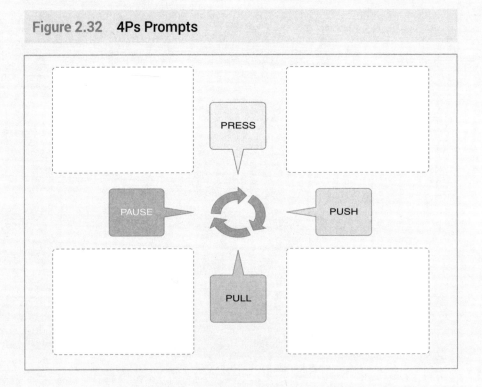

Figure 2.33   4Ps Example

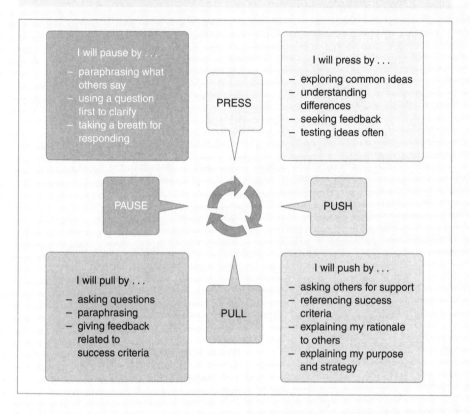

- -

ACTIVITY 2.6
ACTIVATION ACTIVITY

Let's go back to Mrs. Gomez's second-grade class, where learners are focused on the task of growth in their learning. When Mrs. Gomez's students begin their daily learning, they create a plan of action for enhancing their learning for the day. Figure 2.34 illustrates a variety of resources students use to focus their thinking on learning. This enables students to build a sense of orientation and activation.

With a small team of teachers, develop steps that you can take with learners to ensure they are clear on expectations and have resources to support them when planning for the day and when they get stuck in their learning. In essence, how would you promote student efficacy in your classroom?

Figure 2.34   Visual Display of Strategies to Support Learners in Learning

Source: Gomez, J. (2018) Ross School; Ross, CA. Used with permission

NEXT STEPS

- Collect evidence of efficacy using the questions provided earlier in the chapter (Figures 2.4, 2.9, and 2.10).

- Review your own practices and identify whether they reinforce the idea of +1 year of learning across surface, deep, and transfer and develop student individual and collective efficacy.

- Pick one orientation, activation, or collaboration strategy (Visual Resources, Triads, and Agreements/Protocols) and implement with your class.

- Showcase that strategy with other colleagues and to other students. Have each group discuss the similarities and differences in these routines from routines they currently use.

Chapter 3

PLANNING FOR IMPACT

"There should never be a need for the teacher to think
of ways to inject more thinking into the curriculum. That
would be like trying to inject more aerobic exercise into
the lives of Sherpa porters."

—Carl Bereiter, 2002

In 2017, Steven Spielberg was interviewed about his illustrious
career as a director in Hollywood. In the beginning of the HBO
documentary, *Spielberg* (Lacy, Levin, Pildes, & Lacy, 2017), he states,

*Every time I start a new scene, I'm nervous. I've never heard the
lines spoken before. I don't know what I'm going to think when I hear
the lines. I don't know what I'm going to tell the actors, I don't know
where I'm going to put the camera, every time it's the same but I will
tell you it's the greatest feeling in the world . . . the more I'm feeling
confident and secure about something the less I'm going to put out.
The more I'm feeling 'Uh oh, this could be a major problem,' I'm
going to work overtime to meet the challenge and get the job done.*

Example after example of this challenge is illustrated in the 2017 documentary, including Mr. Spielberg's first major motion picture, *Jaws*. Weeks past the deadline, the robotic shark in the repair shop, the script continually being revised, he and many others thought his first major film was far from being a blockbuster and, in fact, on the verge of a disaster. However, these situations gave him the opportunity to improvise and problem solve—he developed the music we know of today that built the suspense because the shark was absent for the majority of the film. Mr. Spielberg had drafted a script, but he left himself room to improvise and adapt while he was filming. He kept the most important part of the story: the story arc. A story arc is essentially ensuring that a story has a setup (establishing the plot and characters), the confrontation (the dilemma(s) that characters face), and the resolution (how the dilemma between or among characters is resolved). In this chapter, I argue that we can use that Spielberg magic to effectively and efficiently focus our planning time on those few items that are essential to move learning forward and then redirect the majority of our time on teaching and adapting to student learning demands.

The available research backs up my hunch that the most effective use of our time as educators is to focus on instructional interventions rather than spending a great deal of time on curriculum planning. Hattie's studies of over half a billion students showed that curriculum was not a likely factor in improving student learning more than one year in a given year (Hattie, 2009). Likewise, research from Shirley Clarke (2014) and Dylan Wiliam (2011) emphasize the need of teachers to focus the majority of their time on practices in the classroom that adapt instruction to meet learner's current progress and proficiency. The common influences that moved learning forward were the *actions* of teachers during instruction. As teachers, we are responsible for ensuring the right elements for student learning at surface, deep, and transfer are in place and then move as quickly as possible to engage with learners and finding out what they know in relationship to expectations and intervene accordingly. Stated differently, planning is critical, but we need to reduce our time on initial planning for everything, as this typically forces us to be rigid and stifles our ability to adapt our planning and instruction to student's progress and proficiency throughout a class or unit.

The motto is to "Stay small and stay focused" when planning so that you can concentrate on your impact on students in the classroom.

In order to do this, we need to walk through the core elements of effective planning and then practice creating planning prototypes (initial plans) so that we can enhance our efficiency in planning.

This chapter on unit planning boils down to two key factors: focus and process. In terms of focus, we will anchor our time in planning on the Guiding Actions that enhance student expertise.

When we plan, we need to focus on the following areas:

- **Clarifying** learning intentions and success criteria

- **Challenging** students at surface, deep, and transfer expectations

- **Checking** student performance and **communicating** feedback, sharing ideas, and debating opinions

- Ensuring **cross contexts** are embedded to meet transfer demands

In this chapter, we will review a simplified unit and lesson template that can be initially developed quickly (i.e., within an hour) and is focused on those elements that are essential.

In terms of process, we need to recognize that our plans will always change once students enter the room; however, our expectations should not change—we'll always expect to see one year's growth (or more) in one year's time across the levels of complexity for the knowledge and skills we are developing. As such, we need to change the adage from creating unit and lesson plans that are "etched in stone" to plans "etched in sand." That is, we need to allow for routine prototyping or revisions before, during, and after engaging with students.

Focused Design

The following template and five design steps enable teachers to effectively create unit plans that emphasize the influences that have the greatest impact on student learning (i.e., the 5Cs Guiding Actions defined in Chapter 1) while minimizing the amount of time needed to design a typical unit plan (see Figure 3.1 and Online Resources 7.10 through 7.14).

Figure 3.1   **Unit Planning Template**

Unit Design			
Learning Intention(s)			
I will . . .	•		
Success Criteria			
	Surface	Deep	Transfer
	•	•	•
Student Tasks			
	Surface	Deep	Transfer
	•	•	•
Lessons			
Prior Knowledge	Surface	Deep	Transfer
	•	•	•
Lessons	•	•	•
Cross Context (Transfer)			
Purposeful and Provocative			
Perplexing Problems			
Perspective Laden			

Calendar					
	Monday	**Tuesday**	**Wednesday**	**Thursday**	**Friday**
Week 1	•	•	•	•	•
Week 2	•	•	•	•	•
Week 3	•	•	•	•	•

Unit Planning: Five Design Steps

The following steps enable educators to effectively create a plan for developing student expertise.

> **Step 1:** Develop Learning Intentions and Create Leveled Success Criteria
>
> **Step 2:** Create Student Tasks

Step 3: Generate Cross Context (Transfer) Situations

Step 4: Craft a Calendar

Step 5: Develop Lessons

Step 1. Develop Learning Intentions and Create Leveled Success Criteria

Step 1 is all about clarifying the goals or outcomes of learning for students and ensuring that they recognize what success looks like. We need to first create learning intentions (i.e., goals/outcomes) that require students to develop surface, deep, and transfer-level work. Moreover, regardless of our own clarity around expectations, we have to make sure that students are clear on such expectations.

To create learning intentions that require surface, deep, and transfer-level while ensuring students have the greatest probability of understanding what is expected, teachers should write goals at the transfer level, written in student friendly language. Specifically, this means that we need to use verbs that are at the transfer level (see Figure 3.6) and craft goals that begin with language such as "I will" statements for students to focus on goals they will meet through the unit (see Figure 3.2 for examples).

When creating learning intentions, it is important to remove the contexts, student activities, or tasks. This step ensures teachers and students are clear on the learning expectations rather than task or performance expectations. The point here is to focus the learner's

Figure 3.2   Sample Learning Intentions Stems

Stems	Examples
I will _____.	I will apply energy transference in an ecosystem to novel problems.
I will _____ in order to _____.	I will apply energy transference in ecosystems in order to solve novel problems. [This sample Learning Intention is drawn from the NGSS standard: MS-LS2-3 Develop a model to describe the cycling of matter and flow of energy among living and nonliving parts of an ecosystem.]

mind on what they are learning and separating the context (or situation) and to see that the task is a way of representing that learning. An important adage from Daniel Willingham (2010) comes to mind here and that is "memory is the residue of thought" (p. 41). What students think about is what they will remember. The more we can focus students on the key outcomes they need to learn, the higher likelihood they will remember core content. In addition, one of the key attributes of a student's ability to transfer learning is to recognize how certain knowledge, skills (surface), and principles (deep) can apply across contexts regardless of the context presented. If students see a particular context in the rubric, they will be less likely to separate the content from that context.

Once you create learning intentions, the criteria for success must be established. Figure 3.3 offers a checklist for creating leveled success criteria to enhance student learning. Leveled criteria may be defined as the specific expectations to meet learning intentions at surface, deep, and transfer.

The previous checklist includes the recommendation to remove all situations or contexts out of the criteria. For example, if the learning intention is associated with learning about food chains, then the success criteria should refrain from situations that students will likely encounter with that topic such as wolf reintroduction (species reintroduction), bamboo (invasive species), and DDT (pesticides). This is paramount for ensuring students will be able to transfer their learning to other situations (see Figure 3.4).

Similarly, we want to keep students focused on what they are supposed to learn, not what they need to complete. As with learning intentions, activities and tasks should be outside the purview of success criteria. For example, if a teacher expects students to write a balanced argument (i.e., learning intention) that includes a thesis and opinions on both sides of an argument (success criteria) and they begin by having students brainstorm (activity) the pros and cons for keeping Confederate monuments (context), then they should keep the activities and context separate from the success criteria. Put differently, activities and tasks are ways to showcase learning and should not be included as success criteria (see Figure 3.5).

Success criteria should also map the expectations of learning at surface, deep, and transfer. One way to do this is to draft a set of criteria for reaching the learning intention of the unit or lesson. The companion website at http://resources.corwin.com/Developing ExpertLearners offers a number of additional examples of leveled

Figure 3.3   Checklist for Creating Leveled Success Criteria That Enhance Student Learning

Characteristics of Robust Success Criteria	Checklist Items	Expectation
Transfer	Does the success criteria include contexts or situations? ☐ Yes ☐ No	Contexts or situations should not be part of the success criteria.
Activities and Tasks	Does the success criteria include activities or tasks? ☐ Yes ☐ No If they do, remove the activities and tasks from the criteria unless they are part of the learning intention. (For example, if students are expected to learn how to write a persuasive essay, then this would be included in the success criteria.)	Activities and tasks should be removed from success criteria unless tasks are stated in the learning intentions.
Complexity	Does the success criteria align with the levels of learning (surface, deep, and transfer)? ☐ Yes ☐ No	Success criteria should be aligned to levels of complexity.
Flexibility	Does the success criteria include open (tools)/closed (rules) items? ☐ Yes ☐ No	If possible, success criteria should denote open and closed items.
Involvement	Does the success criteria invite student co-construction? ☐ Yes ☐ No	When implementing success criteria, inviting students to co-construct success criteria is recommended.
Connected to Measurement Tools	Do the reporting and scoring tools (such as rubrics) directly align to the learning intentions and success criteria? ☐ Yes ☐ No	All reporting, scoring, and grading systems should be directly related to success criteria.

Figure 3.4   Separating Leveled Success Criteria From Contexts

Recommended	Not Recommended
Learning Intention: I will apply the transfer of energy in an ecosystem to various contexts.	Learning Intention: I will apply the transfer of energy in an ecosystem to wolf reintroduction.
Success Criteria • Define food chains, food webs, ecosystems. • Relate food chains and food webs. • Apply the conception of species reintroduction to an ecosystem.	Success Criteria • Define the food chains, food webs, and ecosystems of Yellowstone National Park. • Relate the food chains and food webs of Yellowstone National Park. • Apply the conception of wolf reintroduction in Yellowstone National Park.

Figure 3.5   Separating Leveled Success Criteria From Tasks and Activities

Recommended	Not Recommended
Learning Intention: I will write a balanced argument.	Learning Intention: I will write a balanced argument for or against the preservation of Confederate monuments built in the 1960s.
Success Criteria • Students define opinions for and against an issue. • Students create a rationale for an opinion.	Success Criteria • Students brainstorm reasons for and against the preservation of Confederate monuments built in the 1960s. • Students create a poster that illustrates the relationship between reasons for each opinion.

success criteria (see Online Resources 7.1 through 7.9 for Success Criteria examples). In addition, the appendix offers an alternative development process for success criteria (see Resource 6.8 at the end of the book). Next, using Figure 3.6, educators can link verbs to each criteria that can then be categorized into surface-, deep-, or transfer-level expectations. Figure 3.7 provides an example of success criteria aligned to surface, deep, and transfer expectations.

Figure 3.6   Leveled Success Criteria Rhetoric Tool

Surface (One concept, multiple concepts)	Deep (Connects concepts, ideas, and skills)	Transfer (Applies concepts, ideas, and skills)
<ul><li>Name</li><li>Tell</li><li>Restate</li><li>Define</li><li>Describe who, what, where, when, or how</li><li>Identify</li><li>Recall</li><li>Recite</li><li>Recognize</li><li>Label</li><li>Locate</li><li>Match</li><li>Measure</li><li>Solve one-step task</li><li>Use rules</li><li>List several examples</li><li>Describe and explain using context</li><li>Give examples and non-examples</li><li>Perform a procedure</li><li>Summarize</li><li>Estimate</li><li>Use models to perform procedure</li><li>Estimate</li><li>Use models to perform procedure</li><li>Construct simple model</li><li>Solve multiple-step problem</li></ul>	<ul><li>Cite supporting evidence</li><li>Organize</li><li>Outline</li><li>Interpret</li><li>Revise for meaning</li><li>Explain connections or procedures</li><li>Compare</li><li>Contrast</li><li>Synthesize</li><li>Verify</li><li>Show cause and effect</li><li>Analyze</li><li>Argue</li><li>Assess</li><li>Deconstruct</li><li>Draw conclusions</li><li>Extend patterns</li><li>Infer</li><li>Solve non-routine problems</li></ul>	<ul><li>Reorganize into new structure</li><li>Formulate</li><li>Generalize</li><li>Produce and present</li><li>Design and conduct</li><li>Collaborate</li><li>Evaluate</li><li>Critique</li><li>Hypothesize</li><li>Initiate</li><li>Reflect</li><li>Research</li></ul>

Source: Adapted from Figure 3.5 Surface, Deep, Transfer-Level Learning Rhetoric in *Rigorous PBL By Design,* McDowell, 2017; based on personal communication with Larry Ainsworth, 2016

Figure 3.7   Leveled Success Criteria Aligned to Depth of Complexity

- I can use rates and unit rates to solve problems.
- I can express rates and unit rates to solve problems using models, tables, and line drawings.

Surface	Deep	Transfer
• Define *rate, unit rate, unit pricing, ratio, constant speed, average speed.* • Solve unit rate problems using one method. • Describe unit rate problems using a visual representation.	• Relate rate terms. • Solve unit rate problems using different methods (multiplication expression or division expression). • Relate models, tables, and line drawings to unit rate problems.	• Apply models, tables, and line drawings to various contexts in which rates and unit rates are germane.

Source: Rigorous PBL by Design, McDowell (2017)

In certain situations, success criteria should include open (tools to use) and closed (rules to follow) criteria. Open criteria provide options for learners while closed criteria provide very specific non-negotiable expectations. Shirley Clarke (2014) offers several examples of open and closed success criteria in her book *Outstanding Formative Assessment,* including critical prompts to support teacher design and student discussions. Figure 3.8 offers several examples.

The success criteria checklist (Figure 3.3) also requires interaction between the teacher and students. The notion is for teachers to think about how students could identify success criteria or break down larger success criteria so that students are involved in the process of identifying excellence at the beginning of the unit (see Figure 3.9). Three strategies to consider are

- Develop prompts for starting the unit with a hook and entry event

- Review an assessment

- Share successful examples

Figure 3.8   Open and Closed Success Criteria Examples

Level of Complexity			
Learning Intention	Surface	Deep	Transfer
Math: To apply the addition of two digit numbers	Open: Choose from . . . • A mental method • Using a number line • The column method • Adding tens first, then units, then both together	Open: Choose from . . . • Two or more methods	Open: Choose from . . . • A set of units to develop and solve problems
	Closed: Remember to . . . • Add the ones place before the tens	Closed: Remember to . . . • Combine technique to solve given problem	Closed: Remember to . . . • Apply multiple methods to various problems
	Universal: Every time we . . . • Solve a problem we show each step • Check our answer by asking a peer	Universal: Every time we . . . • Solve a problem we show each step • Check our answer by asking a peer	Universal: Every time we . . . • Solve a problem we see how the math is similar across contexts and situations
ELA: To write a persuasive essay	Open: Choose . . . • A medium (newspaper, conclusion of a scientific paper) • A different ending (moral, cliff-hanger)	Open: Choose . . . • A medium and an appropriate ending	Open: Choose from . . . • The context/situation

(Continued)

Figure 3.8   (Continued)

Level of Complexity			
Learning Intention	**Surface**	**Deep**	**Transfer**
	Closed: Remember to . . . • Include a title • Create an opinion • Provide evidence	Closed: Remember to . . . • Relate the title to the author's opinion • Connect author's opinion to counter opinions	Closed: Remember to . . . • Use surface and deep criteria in different contexts
	Universal: Every time we . . . • Write we use appropriate grammar (see other success criteria) • Write we give and receive feedback	Universal: Every time we . . . • Write we use appropriate grammar (see other success criteria) • Write we give and receive feedback	Universal: Every time we . . . • Write we use appropriate grammar (see other success criteria) • Write we give and receive feedback

The next chapter provides a series of routines to get students involved in generating success criteria. To complete the success criteria checklist, all marking, assessment, reporting, and grading approaches should be directly linked to the success criteria of learning. The key point here is to align a simplified scoring method to the success criteria along the depth of complexity you have created.

Though there are many ways to assess student learning, this text offers a one-point rubric (see Figure 3.10 and Figure 3.11) that assigns a point if students meet the success criteria (shown in the middle column). Teachers and students use the "Strengths" column to list areas of success while the "opportunities" column is used to list areas of improvement and potential next steps.

Step 2. Create Student Tasks

Once learning intentions and success criteria have been created, we need means for students to develop and showcase their understanding.

Figure 3.9   Success Criteria Co-Construction

Strategy	The Strategy in Action—Ask the Students . . .
Develop prompts for starting the unit with a hook and entry event	• After watching the YouTube video, what key questions emerge for you? What are we going to study? If we were charged with solving this problem, what appears to be critical for success? • After reading the memo, what does success look like for us? • Russia started the Cold War. What do we need to know to support or defend this statement?
Review an assessment	• What do students need to know and be able to do to master the questions on this assessment? • What appears to be the main theme or topic associated with this assessment? What does success look like to meet the demands of this assessment? • After reviewing the performance of two students from last year, can you explain what went wrong?
Share successful examples	• After looking at the following two exemplars, do they both seem to be of the same quality? How do they relate? How are they similar? How would you improve their work? What seems to be the most successful aspects of the work? • One of the exemplars has a major challenge and one does not have that challenge. Can you find it? Why is X a challenge? • In the following solutions, the students used more than one strategy to solve the problem. Why? Is that required? • Here are four exemplars. Can you put them in order from best to least successful? Talk with the person next to you about your rationale for ranking them this way. • One of the exemplars is not an effective example. Can you find it and discuss why with your partner?

Figure 3.10   One-Point Rubric

Strengths (areas of success shown on the assignment)	Success Students Need to Meet in Order to Earn the Point	Opportunities (list areas of potential improvement and potential next steps)
	Surface •	
	Deep •	
	Transfer •	

Figure 3.11   **One-Point Rubric Example**

Strengths	Success Criteria	Opportunities
	Surface • Writes the title of a book as a question • Lists several examples of comparing connectives • Lists several examples of contrasting connectives • Lists several high percentage findings for one side of an argument	
	Deep • Combines contrasting and comparing connectives to opinions • Combines high percentage findings for or against an opinion • Summarizes opinion in the closing	
	Transfer • Applies other rhetorical devices to make an argument (logos, ethos, pathos) • Applies other solution criteria of a balanced argument to a new situation	

We do this by identifying the tasks or performances students will complete. Figure 3.12 offers a checklist that assists in developing these instruments.

Figure 3.12   **Checklist: Characteristics of Robust Tasks**

Characteristics of Robust Tasks	
Depth of Complexity	Tasks are aligned to surface, deep, and transfer. ☐ Yes ☐ No
Cognitively Challenging	The majority of tasks require students to write, read, and present to and with others to demonstrate their understanding. ☐ Yes ☐ No
Connection to Prior Knowledge	Tasks require students to connect prior knowledge (past experience and levels of complexity). ☐ Yes ☐ No

Focusing on What Matters

Kelley Miller, Academic Coach
Silverado Middle School
Napa, California

I love the simplicity of a to-do list. I'd even argue that it adds clarity to the classroom. When given a list of tasks to accomplish, students and their parents know exactly what they need to check off the list to get an A. Likewise, I like knowing exactly how much work I need to assign and how much time I'll need to give students to get it all done. Crossing things off a list makes sense for any time-pressed teacher. I have learned, however, that it can be a symptom of thinking about the wrong thing.

Graham Nuthall's research confirms what I frequently see at my school: buzz between students naturally gravitates to "What number are you on?" and "How long did it take you?" I don't consider that a fault of our students; it's just a fact. Likewise, my planning time often begins with logistics: how much time, how many points, and which favorite activities should be modified from last year? Those parameters are important. But if my class is just a sum of activities, how do my students and I know if real learning has occurred?

I knew I needed to make a change when I realized that my students could not use a skill set that they'd learned when it was in a new context. A few years ago, I meticulously planned a month-long explanatory reading and writing project for my eighth graders. They filled in graphic organizers, researched, and wrote essays. However, when our standardized test asked them to do the exact same thing regarding a new topic, many of them felt paralyzed. My students had spent the previous month doing all the things I had asked them to do but, because I failed to emphasize what we were *learning* over what we were *doing*, their thinking remained tied to a single context.

After that experience, I started making attempts to bring clarity of learning intentions to the forefront in my classroom. I am a wife and a mother, so re-designing the rest of the year's lesson plans was not a realistic solution. But I discovered almost immediately that making small shifts made a significant impact on how my students and I thought about what we were in doing in class each day.

It started with reading a novel. Before we began the novel, I explained our learning intentions: We were going to get really good at discussing theme, using textual evidence to support writing about theme, and identifying how various other elements of fiction related to theme . . . and we were going to

(Continued)

(Continued)

use this novel to get us there. (It's not the strongest way to "sell" a novel to teenagers, but it was a book they love, so I had wiggle room.) I dedicated an entire bulletin board to a chart of what our learning would look like at surface, deep, and transfer levels. Moreover, I frequently brought students' attention back to that chart as we went through different activities to show them how what we were *doing* gave us space to practice what we were *learning*. Those learning intentions eventually became our rubric after reading the novel, and students knew exactly how they'd be expected to show their learning.

Frequently reminding students of what we were learning helped keep *me* on track as well. If an activity didn't support the learning we'd been discussing every day, why were we doing it? Certain assignments were given higher priority under that lens; others were discarded. Those discussions also helped me prioritize what went into the gradebook. Were students able to demonstrate transfer-level knowledge? Where did I need to spend energy (and time) on a re-teach?

I continued those small shifts on subsequent projects throughout the year. In each case, it only took small adjustments to keep learning intentions at the center of our work. Students still answered writing prompts, read assigned pages, and engaged in collaborative discussions—they still did activities—but there was a new transparency, for me and for them, regarding why we were doing them. Talking about what we were learning, measuring our progress, and looking to see where we still needed to go became a more natural part of our culture. That year's cohort left me feeling confident that, in my classroom, we had honestly and visibly engaged in the business of learning.

In a broader context, the principle of keeping learning intentions paramount is no different for young learners than it is for adults. When I facilitate professional development, I keep in mind that we want to know why what we're doing is relevant, and as leaders in the classroom, we want to make sure we are pointing our students and ourselves in the right direction. There's no time to be wasted on guessing what we're supposed to be learning.

I still love a good list. But now I know how powerful a list can be when it prioritizes what we will be learning over what we will be doing. Learners naturally let their thoughts dwell on the task at hand, whether they are preschoolers or seasoned educators. I try to draw clearer lines connecting the tasks with the learning, so we all can walk away confident that we're thinking about the right thing. The change is small, but it's simple. And I'm learning a lot from that.

Examples of tasks aligned to the aforementioned checklist (Figure 3.12) are shown in Figure 3.13.

Figure 3.13 Task Examples

Depth of Complexity	Surface	Deep	Transfer
Cognitively Challenging	• Create a list. • Draft an outline. • Solve a problem. • Read a passage.	• Develop a concept/mind map. • Draft a piece of writing. • Solve problems with multiple strategies/relating concepts. • Annotate passages with inferences. • Build a model.	• Create and present a new model. • Produce and present solutions to problems across contexts. • Design and conduct tests. • Evaluate own work and that of others.

Separating Success Criteria From Tasks

Aaron Eisberg, Coordinator
Center for Excellence, Napa New Tech High School
Napa, California

One of the early mistakes I made when I first wrote the "Medical Intern's Project," a spotlight project for Buck Institute for Education (BIE), was that my students were unclear on what success looked like in the project. From a teacher's perspective, I thought I had been clear. I thought to myself, "I taught the content to them, they should have known the difference between arteries and veins!" The problem was my own lack of knowledge and experience with success criteria. I unknowingly focused student success on the graphic organizer and then on coloring the diagram red and blue rather than asking them to focus on understanding the similarities and differences between arteries and veins.

(Continued)

(Continued)

I noticed that students were seeking feedback on completion of tasks and constantly looking for me to tell them whether they had met my task-based expectations. Time and time again I could see that students were not focusing on the actual knowledge and skills I wanted them to learn through the tasks without specific prompting, tools, and redirection.

In the early phase of our learning, it was a challenge to separate success in learning and success in completing a task. Additionally, I struggled with helping students differentiate the more complex ideas from the more elementary ones. Then we had breakthrough. I started to create leveled success criteria at surface, deep, and transfer levels and to remove all tasks from my rubrics (i.e., success criteria). From this point onward, when I created tasks (ways learners could demonstrate their knowledge), I asked myself "What are the best ways learners can show me their knowledge at surface, deep, and transfer levels?" This process allowed me to step back from all my tasks (e.g., the students' oral presentations) and get to my central goal of learning (e.g., students are able to answer the question, "How are the body systems dependent upon each other and how might an alteration to part of that system impact how the body functions?").

In the past, when I rolled the project out, every learner thought success in the project was presenting to a panel of nurses and doctors about a patient. By separating clarity of success (understanding how different body systems interact with each other and how alterations in body systems would affect the body) and the tasks in which they could share their knowledge (individual writing and group oral presentation), learners were able to understand and learn the content knowledge at deeper levels. Nowadays, the design of the project allows for more student voice and student choice, more clarity of success, which has led to more student success in the project and, more importantly, in their learning.

Step 3. Generate Transfer Situations

Figure 3.14 illustrates a series of success criteria teachers should consider when engaging students in developing the knowledge and skills necessary to meet transfer-level work.

When coupled, the elements of transfer tasks (purposeful/provocative, perplexing, and perspective-laden) provide students with a high degree of relevance to their learning, compassion for others, a recognition of bias, and involvement in making an impact in the world. Let's look at each of the transfer-level criteria at a deeper level.

Figure 3.14   Success Criteria for Transfer Tasks

Criteria	Description
Purposeful and Provocative Problems	*Students must work together to address meaningful (and often charged) situations that have the potential to impact others.* • Identify problems that are purposeful and challenging for people to consider.
Perplexing Problems	*Students must work together to apply surface- and deep-level content knowledge and skills within and between contexts while handling changes in various dynamics of problems over time.* • Identify changes in the problem situation that would impact the solution. • Identify changes in the problem situation that would require new or additional tasks. • Identify changes in the context that require transferring knowledge to other situations.
Perspective-Laden Problems	*Students must work together to understand and apply various values, beliefs, and perspectives inherent within the construct of the problem to create solutions.* • Identify various values, perspectives, and beliefs that are connected to this context/issue. • Identify biases that are at play in the situation.

Purposeful and Provocative Problems

Perplexing problems are exponentially more interesting to students when they relate to their lives and the lives of others. Teachers often demonstrate this by forming a question that drives students to pursue learning content as a means to address a genuine question facing society, students, and/or species. Here are but a few examples of questions that may drive student learning:

- *Should Confederate monuments built during the 1960s be removed from local, state, and federal properties?*

- *Should entrance exams for advanced placement courses be removed from school policies?*

- *Should creationism be taught side by side with evolution in science classes?*

- *How do we reconcile alleged bullying in the second-grade classroom?*

- *Should corporations like Facebook be regulated by the government?*

Each of these questions conjures up emotions, strikes at a level of relevance for learners, and inspires action.

Perplexing Problems

In *Visible Learning for Teachers*, John Hattie (2012) wrote that *"Too often, students are asked to relate and extend with minimal ideas on which to base this task-leading to impoverished deeper learning. . . . The claim here, instead, is that teachers must know at what phase of learning the student is best invested—in learning more surface ideas, and moving from the surface to a deeper relating and extending of these ideas"* (p. 95). As discussed earlier in this chapter, creating leveled-success criteria at surface, deep, and transfer is critical. Moreover, we need to ensure students are accessing and using surface and deep knowledge and skills when solving transfer-level problems. One way to do this is to instill change(s) in transfer-level tasks.

In real-world situations, new issues emerge (e.g., fall in gas prices, a storm, introduction of a new species to an island), new deadlines or task expectations are required (e.g., back up literature review, Op-Ed), and at times, there are changes in the problems students are trying to solve (e.g., adding onto the area of a deck to reducing the area of a backyard for a dog house). Figure 3.15 offers a series of strategies that compels students to address transfer-level tasks. Figure 3.16 offers a plethora of examples about how these strategies operate in the classroom.

Figure 3.15   Defining Elements of Perplexing Problems

Strategies	Description	Examples
Twists	• Provide students with changes in expectations of the tasks they are working to complete.	• Instead of creating a persuasive essay, you are now writing a script to convey the same message.
Turns	• Provide students with a change in the context or situation they are currently working in.	• Instead of increasing the area of a deck, we need to reduce the area.
Sequels	• Design a new problem within a new context (requires same content, could include prior knowledge explored in class).	• Instead of reintroducing a species into an ecosystem, you are now charged with eradicating an invasive species.

Figure 3.16 Examples of Twists, Turns, and Sequels

Changes in the Problem Situation That Require New/Additional Tasks (twists)	Changes in the Problem Situation That Would Impact the Solution (turns)	Various Perspectives and Beliefs That are Connected to This Context/Issue (sequels)
• The non-profit group has unfortunately lost its funding and is no longer able to bring a group out to see your presentation. We would ask that you submit a written summary of your conclusions.	• The number of articles posted on (this topic) lack the nuance we would like to see. Please conclude your essay with a more engaging ending.	• Design a solution for removing a population rather than reintroducing a species.
• The group has formed a broader conclusion involving _____, which is _____, and we would like you to provide a critique of this decision.	• We just received word that we are required to no longer take accumulated interest for granted. Initiate a means for addressing this new wrinkle.	• Craft a critique for how your conclusions would relate to the following situation _____.
• We have run out of _____ and expect you to conduct the investigation without this resource.	• The business partner is concerned that fuel costs will be higher if we ignore air resistance. Reorganize your solution based on this customer need.	
• The following situation has come to light that may impact your conclusions.		
• We are less than confident in the conclusions that have been brought forward. We will be asking several questions and expect thorough responses to ensure our confidence in this project.		
• We are expecting that your presentation includes multiple ways of demonstrating your solution.		
• We have included a few more elements in our presentation requirements including formulating hypotheses to your responses. Please include hypotheses to your decisions, potential limitations, and means for testing your conclusions.		

The appendix includes additional resources for developing purposeful and perplexing strategies (See Resource 6.9a).

Perspective-Laden Problems

Incorporating various perspectives and beliefs to a problem or issue is essential to supporting students in meeting transfer-level expectations. Likewise, there is a genuineness or realism to a problem when multiple sides are explored. Figure 3.17 illustrates a series of strategies that teachers may use to ensure students are considering various opinions and perspectives of those impacted by a problem. Figure 3.18 offers a series of activities teachers could use with students to explore and address biases.

Figure 3.17   Perspective Strategies

	Description	Example
Flipping Perspectives	• Students engage in exploring the perspectives of groups that are being impacted by decisions and a particular type of political, social, or economic standing to advocate for a different solution.	• Students review the political, social, and economic challenges faced by the Osage and other Native American tribes during the Allotment Act. • Students then relate such actions of a government to contemporary society.
Plus Sum	• Students take the perspective that a solution must offer maximum benefit to all groups while minimizing negative effects.	• Students analyze a series of solutions to a problem and assess those solutions relative to all constituency groups affected. • Students then identify a solution that provides the greatest compromise and ultimately the greatest positive effect for all groups.
Challenging Assumptions	• Students generate a set of assumptions that may be influencing or deemphasizing particular research, people, beliefs, perspectives, and solutions.	• Students generate a list of assumptions that may be guiding particular solutions forward for specific groups of people. • These assumptions are then scrutinized by historical data, empirical research, and student led case studies.

Figure 3.18   Tackling Bias

Bias	Description	Examples
Loss aversion	People's tendency to prefer avoiding losses to acquiring equivalent gain.	• Have students debate how decisions are altered if resources or time are augmented.
Value attribution	Value attribution describes our tendency to imbue people or objects with certain qualities based on perceived value rather than on objective data.	• Ask students to write down what they like (e.g., hobbies, movies, books, social media) and what they value (e.g., honesty, humor, respect). Next ask students to jot down what they are like on a daily basis (i.e., Are you big picture or more detail oriented? Do you like to work independently or collaboratively?). Next give them a profile of someone without objective data of their quality for a job interview. Ask them if this is someone they would be interested in talking with about a job for a company.
Diagnosis bias (confirmation bias)	Refers to our propensity to label people, ideas, or objects based on our initial opinions of them—and our inability to reconsider these judgements once we have made them.	• Have students make a decision about a topic and then have them read two articles (one confirming and one countering their beliefs). Next, ask them to define which has a higher level of reliability and validity. Ensure that both studies have a high level of research quality.
Overconfidence	Refers to our high level of confidence in our judgment relative to the facts.	• Have students review a series of effective and ineffective decisions others have made in the past. Have them identify why there are differences between effective and ineffective decisions. Next, tell them that others believed that the effective decisions were based on their "gut" instinctive decisions and poor decisions were based on external factors. Ask them how they would coach those individuals toward a better understanding of overconfidence bias. Finally, ask students to identify what they can do to ensure they don't succumb to overconfidence bias.

The appendix offers additional resources for developing transfer tasks including tools for evaluating transfer tasks (see Resources 6.9b and 6.9c).

Step 4. Craft a Calendar

Step 4 is for teachers to craft a tentative timeline for sequencing student learning of surface, deep, and transfer learning (see Figure 3.19). The calendar is typically broken into three sections:

- **Unit Launch**—Day 1 through 3 provide students with a general map of the next several days or weeks along with a clear sense of expectations (i.e., learning intentions and success criteria), their current performance (via pre-assessment), and next steps that are required to meet expectations.

- **Learning Sequence**—Day 3 through 10 (or more) are associated with lessons at surface, deep, and transfer to build students understanding at all levels of complexity.

- **Unit Conclusion**—conclusion of the unit typically includes a post-assessment, reflections, and potentially additional transfer-level tasks (see next chapter).

Step 5. Develop Lessons

Lessons are the daily scaffolds that lead up to meeting unit-level expectations. By the nature of its design, Figure 3.1, the Unit Planning

Figure 3.19   Calendar Example

Calendar					
	Monday	Tuesday	Wednesday	Thursday	Friday
Week 1	• Pre-assessment • Review learning intentions and success criteria	• Surface-level lesson	• Surface-level lesson	• Deep lesson	• Deep lesson
Week 2	• Deep lesson	• Transfer lesson	• Post-assessment	• Transfer lesson	• Reflections • Feedback to teacher

Template, focuses educators on developing all of the step-by-step scaffolds needed to complete the unit. Figure 3.20 provides an optional lesson plan structure that teachers could use if they want to explicitly plan for each day (Figure 3.21 provides an example of a lesson plan). It is important to emphasize that this template, like the unit templates, are just that, templates. The template should not be the focus but rather the focus should be on ensuring students learn at substantial levels (see Online Resource 7.11 for a template and see Online Resource 7.13 for an example).

Regardless of whether the template is used, effective lessons need to be aligned to complexity levels and student prior knowledge (including student misconceptions, student prior understanding, and paradoxes). A simple way of thinking about daily lessons is the 3Ls: Leverage, Link, and Lift. *Leverage* refers to a teacher's approach to connecting students' prior knowledge (current understanding, misconceptions, and paradoxes) to the learning intentions and success criteria of the unit and the specific lesson embedded within the unit. *Link* refers to a teacher's approach to connecting the best possible feedback and instructional and learning strategies to support student learning. As discussed in Chapter 1 (See Figure 1.1), there are certain strategies that have a higher probability of supporting student learning at each level of complexity (i.e., surface, deep, and transfer). During this time, students are working with peers to

Figure 3.20   Example of a Daily Lesson Structure

Strategies	Examples of the Strategies
Leverage	• Review the learning intention of the unit • Review the success criteria for the lesson • Review student current knowledge/ideas/questions
Link	• Align feedback, instruction, and learning strategies to surface, deep, and transfer • Align tasks to the surface, deep, and transfer
Lift	• Summarize student learning relative to learning intentions and success criteria • Review individual performance and next steps in learning

accomplish various tasks to learn and demonstrate their learning to others. Finally, *lift* are the routines that teachers and peers use to summarize their learning, review their performance, and discuss next steps. The word lift is used as a metaphor for "lifting up" or inspecting their learning and examining their performance and next steps.

Figure 3.21 provides an overview of a unit on the movement of matter among plants, animals, decomposers, and the environment to solve environment problems. Notice the success criteria for the entire unit are provided and cover surface, deep, and transfer criteria.

Planning Process

The previous section illustrates a series of important considerations when designing a unit for learning (not a unit of instruction!). As we develop a unit for learning, we need to develop a process where we create multiple prototypes and incorporate feedback from others (via Figure 3.1). This requires initial development of a plan, followed by immediate feedback (see Figure 3.22), and implementation, again followed up by immediate feedback. The following brief subsection outlines these steps in detail.

Figure 3.22 outlines a one-page planning template that covers six phases that ensure the highest probability of enhancing student learning. Each phase is described below.

Phase I: Sketch Initial Draft (Steps 1–3 of a Unit for Learning)

Phase II: Feedback and Adjustment

Phase III: Sketch Initial Draft (Steps 4–5 of a Unit for Learning)

Phase IV: Feedback and Adjustment

Phase V: Formative Implementation (during teaching and learning process)

Phase VI: Reflective Feedback and Adjustment

To plan effectively and efficiently, teachers should consider using the Developing Expert Learners (DEL) Planning Process shown in Figures 3.22 and 3.23. The DEL Planning Process requires multiple check-ins with colleagues to get feedback before, during, and after the unit is implemented in the classroom. One way to ensure an efficient

Figure 3.21 **Unit and Lesson Example**

Description of Unit	On the first day of class, students were shown an image of sea lampreys and asked if these animals should be removed from the Great Lakes. Next, the students were given the learning intention of the unit and the success criteria (see below). On Day 2, the teacher designed a lesson for supporting students in defining key terms that are needed to move to more complex outcomes.

Learning Intention: I will apply the concepts of movement of matter among plants, animals, decomposers, and the environment to solve environmental problems.

Success Criteria

Surface	Deep	Transfer
I will . . .	I will . . .	I will . . .
• Define food chains, food webs, ecosystems • Describe a healthy ecosystem • List types of organisms (producers, consumers, decomposers) • Describe introduction and reintroduction of a species	• Relate food chains and food webs • Relate types of organisms and their role in food chains and food webs • Relate introduction or reintroduction to the balance of ecosystems • Relate the complexity of food chains/webs to the health of an ecosystem	• Propose a solution to an invasive species that is affecting the health of an ecosystem

Leverage	• Students will be given a list of statements related to food chains, food webs, invasive species, desirable exotics, ecosystems, and re/introduction, types of animals (producers, consumers, decomposers). Students will indicate whether each statement is true or false. The teacher will then ask students to explain their answers to their learning partners and then will call on students to ask them to discuss their thinking. • Students will then review the surface success criteria by using the accordion method (see Figure 4.2). Students then review an exemplar outline and are tasked with identifying how that outline meets the criteria.
Link	• The teacher reviews each term with students and models the creation of an outline that shows the relationship between the various constructs. The students give and receive feedback on the teacher's outline of the key terms. • The students then have an opportunity to craft an outline of their own. • The students give and receive feedback on each other's outlines.
Lift	• Students examine their learning for the day and what next steps they need to take. (This process is required for every student regardless of their performance toward success criteria.)

process is to use the one-page template illustrated in Figure 3.1 and to use protocols to structure the conversation between the teacher writing the unit and receiving feedback and colleagues giving feedback to the teacher. Protocols are simply processes for structuring conversations. We use protocols in schools to ensure that we are listening to others and giving and receiving feedback without a strong emotional response when hearing information that evaluates or criticizes our work. The mantra should always be "Soft on people, hard on content." You can find useful examples of school communication protocols in the appendix—for example, Resource 6.5 Constructivist Tuning Protocol, Resource 6.6 Learning Dilemma Protocol, and Resource 6.7 Constructivist Listening Protocol.

Figure 3.22   DEL Planning Process—Steps

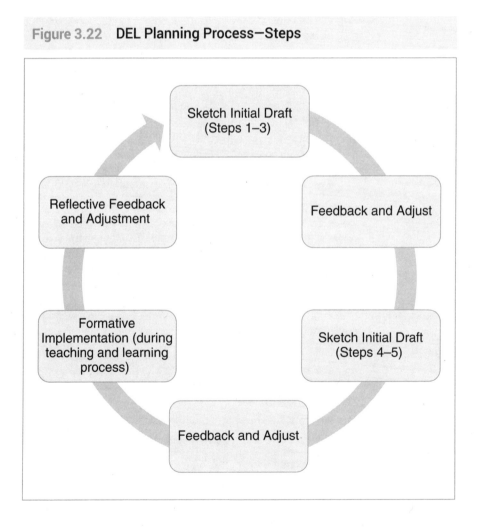

Figure 3.23 DEL Planning Process—Actions

Sketch Initial Draft (Steps 1–3)	Teachers draft learning intentions, success criteria, and tasks.
Feedback and Adjust	• A team of teachers reviews the learning intentions, success criteria, and tasks and offers feedback on the alignment of learning intentions to success criteria and to ensure that tasks are clearly separate from established success criteria. • One protocol that is beneficial during this phase is Resource 6.7, the Constructivist Listening Protocol.
Sketch Initial Draft (Steps 4–5)	• After receiving feedback, the teacher finalizes the unit of learning by completing Steps 3–5. Once these steps have been drafted, the teacher brings the unit back to the team of teachers for feedback.
Feedback and Adjust	• A team of teachers review the cross context (transfer) situations and create a calendar for the unit of learning. • Repeat the Constructivist Listening Protocol (Resource 6.7).
Adjust Plan	• Based on feedback after the first two cycles of input, the teacher adjusts the plan and then implements with learners.
Formative Implementation (during teaching and learning process)	• During the teaching and learning process, the teacher brings student evidence of learning, their own opinions on efficacy of the unit of learning, and any adjustments they made during instruction. • A protocol that works well here would be Resource 6.6, the Learning Dilemma protocol, to support the teacher in their learning.
Reflective Feedback and Adjustment	• After the unit of learning has concluded, the teacher will make final adjustments and may bring their changes to the teachers to re-engage in a Learning Dilemma protocol (Resource 6.6) or a Constructivist Listening protocol (Resource 6.7).

Conclusion

The critical message from this chapter is to design units of learning effectively by anchoring the design to a few elements of learning that are essential to enable students to grow across surface, deep, and transfer expectations. Additionally, this chapter emphasized the need to design units efficiently by going through the prototype process above.

REFLECTION QUESTIONS

- How is the approach of unit and lesson design in this book different from your current practice? What do you see as the pros and cons of this approach?

- What step appears to be the most challenging to your current practice? Why?

  1. Develop Learning Intentions and Create Leveled Success Criteria

  2. Create Tasks

  3. Generate Cross Context (Transfer) Situations

  4. Craft a Calendar

  5. Develop Lessons

- How is the approach of unit and lesson planning in this book different from your current practice? What do you see as the pros and cons of this approach?

- What step appears to be the most challenging to your current practice of planning? Why?

  1. Sketch Initial Draft (Steps 1–3)

  2. Feedback and Adjust

  3. Sketch Initial Draft (Steps 4–5)

  4. Feedback and Adjust

  5. Formative Implementation (during teaching and learning process)

  6. Reflective Feedback and Adjustment

ACTIVITIES

ACTIVITY 3.1
ETCHED IN SAND

Using the template shown in Figure 3.22, draft five unit plans in a matter of 60 to 90 minutes and receive feedback from colleagues. When receiving feedback, consider using Resources 6.5, 6.6, and 6.7 in the appendix at the back of the book. After receiving feedback from colleagues, make revisions and implement the lessons with your students.

- -

ACTIVITY 3.2
TUNE IT UP

Practice creating three to five learning intentions and success criteria and having colleagues provide feedback against the checklist in Figure 3.3 (consider using Resources 6.5, 6.6, and 6.7 for guidance on the feedback process).

- -

ACTIVITY 3.3
PROTOCOL PRACTICE

Practice using the protocols (Resources 6.5, 6.6, and 6.7) by evaluating and giving feedback to the project shown in Figure 3.24.

Figure 3.24   Unit Planning Example

Unit Design: Silent Spring?	
Learning Intention(s)	
I will …	1. *apply a scientific explanation based on evidence for the role of photosynthesis in the cycling of matter to a real-world situation.*
I will …	2. *understand the effects of resource availability on organisms and populations of organisms in an ecosystem.*
I will …	3. *adopt one of many competing design solutions for maintaining biodiversity and healthy ecosystems.*
I will …	4. *apply my understanding of local plants to solutions that ensure healthy ecosystems and biodiversity.*

(Continued)

Figure 3.24   (Continued)

Success Criteria			
	Surface	Deep	Transfer
	<ul><li>Define photosynthesis and transpiration.</li><li>Know the basic parts of a tree and its functions.</li><li>Define leaf morphology.</li></ul>	<ul><li>Relate photosynthesis and transpiration.</li><li>Compare and contrast the basic parts of a tree and its functions.</li><li>Link photosynthesis and transpiration to the basic parts of a tree and leaf morphology.</li></ul>	<ul><li>Apply the role of the structures and the purpose of photosynthesis to a real-world situation.</li></ul>
	<ul><li>Define the following: food webs, succession, competition, adaptation, symbiosis, trophic levels, organisms, and populations.</li></ul>	<ul><li>Compare and contrast the following terms: food webs, succession, competition, adaptation, symbiosis, trophic levels, energy transfer, organisms, and populations.</li></ul>	<ul><li>Using evidence, apply how energy transfer influences populations and organisms.</li></ul>
	<ul><li>Identify common control techniques for removing pathogens and insects in forests.</li><li>Identify common pathogens and insects in the forest.</li></ul>	<ul><li>Relate common control techniques for removing pathogens and insects in forests.</li></ul>	<ul><li>Apply common control techniques for removing pathogens and insects in forests.</li></ul>
	<ul><li>Identify the four most common forest plant communities in California and their ranges.</li><li>Identify coastal redwood and Douglas fir.</li><li>Define leaf morphology.</li></ul>	<ul><li>Identify the four most common forest plant communities in California and their ranges.</li><li>Identify coastal redwood and Douglas fir.</li></ul>	<ul><li>Apply understanding of local forest plant communities to a real-world problem.</li></ul>

Student Tasks			
	Surface	Deep	Transfer
	• Submits an advanced organizer with supporting material with definitions	• Writes a literature review relating core concepts	• Presents solution to problem presented in class (codifies transfer expectations of all learning goals) • Provides supporting argumentative paper
Lessons			
	Surface	Deep	Transfer
Prior Knowledge	• Students typically understand the idea behind photosynthesis but lack the vocabulary and the process in detail.	• Students have past experiences from observations but often lack the science background in process (scientific method) and content (definitions, cycles).	• Students have presumably not encountered the types of problems they will face in these contexts. But they do have experience solving problems.
Lessons *This example illustrates one lesson example for each complexity level.*	• Leverage: Assess student understanding, review learning intentions and success criteria.	• Leverage: Assess student understanding, review learning intentions and success criteria.	• Leverage: Assess student understanding, review learning intentions and success criteria.

(Continued)

Figure 3.24   (Continued)

	• Link: Provide an advanced organizer with visual, require students to elaborate on core definitions and the process of photosynthesis • Lift: Review key learning	• Link: Present students with multiple scenarios that may disrupt the forest and explain why certain techniques may improve the environment • Lift: Review key learning	• Link: Provide students with multiple scenarios and have students identify potential solutions • Lift: Review key learning

Cross Context (Transfer)

Purposeful and Provocative	Questions or Problems to consider: *How do we balance the immediate needs of humans with the long-term needs of local flora and fauna?* *How does one manage a forest that is suffering from numerous challenges while meeting the needs of humans?*
Perplexing Problems	Cost restrictions to solutions, new factors emerge (new invasive species, change in climate, weather conditions, state, federal, or international policy or political issues emerge)
Perspective-Laden	Logging industry, tourism, federal/state agencies, environmental groups

Calendar

	Monday	Tuesday	Wednesday	Thursday	Friday
Week 1–2	Present Transfer Problem Pre-Assessment	Surface Workshops	Surface Workshops	Surface Workshops	Surface Workshops
Week 2–4	Deep Workshops	Deep Workshops	Deep Workshops	Deep Workshops	Assessment
Week 5–6	Deep Workshops	Transfer Workshops	Presentation	Sequel	Reflection

Six–week example

Leverage	• Review the learning intention of the unit.
	• Review the success criteria for the lesson.
	• Review student current knowledge/ideas/questions.
Link	• Align feedback, instruction, and learning strategies to surface, deep, and transfer.
	• Align tasks to the surface, deep, and transfer.
	• Focuses students on expertise-based strategies.
Lift	• Summarize student learning relative to learning intentions and success criteria.
	• Review individual performance and next steps in learning.
	• Focuses students on efficacy-based strategies.

ACTIVITY 3.4

INSPECTING LEVELED SUCCESS CRITERIA

In the following activity, you will write a learning intention and a set of leveled success criteria. After drafting the success criteria, have a colleague answer the following question regarding your work:

- Are students only shown what they are learning regardless of the context (or situation)? Are students only shown what they will learn regardless of the tasks required?

- Are students shown the expectations of learning across levels of complexity (surface, deep, and transfer)?

DESIGNING LEARNING INTENTIONS AND SUCCESS CRITERIA

Figure 3.25   **Learning Intention and Leveled Success Criteria Template**

Learning Intention: I will . . .		
Surface	Deep	Transfer

Next, redraft the criteria and then consider the following question (this will be discussed in the next chapter):

- How will you actively involve students in understanding and using the success criteria in their learning? How will you support each learner in providing self and peer feedback toward meeting the established leveled success criteria? Hint: Look at Figure 3.9

NEXT STEPS

- Review the unit and lesson plans you are currently using in your classroom. Compare your units/lessons to the five design steps. Next, identify where/how you might make potential shifts in your design to have a greater impact on student learning.

- Draft a series of learning intentions and success criteria (see Activity 3.4) with colleagues.

Chapter 4

TEACHING FOR IMPACT

In our pursuit to developing expert learners we must consider the actions we take on a daily basis to support learning at each level of complexity and in building learners' capacity to take responsibility over their own learning (i.e., orientation, activation, and collaboration). In this chapter, we look at strategies that best move students toward expertise (surface, deep, and transfer). This is accomplished by aligning teacher actions to each level of complexity (i.e., instructional strategies), enabling learners to use learning strategies that support their own learning at each level of complexity, and giving and receiving feedback that has the best chance to move learning forward. This chapter also recommends integrating efficacy-based strategies discussed in Chapter 2, particularly orientation strategies, in the teaching and learning process.

Illuminating the Hidden Understandings of Learners

We often don't see or hear what students are thinking about during our modeling, guided practice, and their independent practice. We are often outside of earshot when they are engaging in informal conversations or working in small groups. This is troubling given that we won't know when students are sharing misinformation about the curriculum with each other or when a fundamental misunderstanding about the material being studied is passed on from student to student.

The role and responsibility of evaluating learning and taking action in light of such data is essential to implementing routines in the classroom. As Nuthall (2007) states,

> Knowing that a student is busily engaged in an activity does not tell you what (or how) the student is learning. You need to know exactly what information or knowledge is engaging the student's mind. To give a simplified example, it is not enough to say that a student learned because the student was busy reading a book unless you also identify what the student was reading and how that content related to what the student already knew . . . What has not changed is the mythical belief that engaging in learning activities (such as listening to teacher talking, discussing the results of an experiment, or writing a report of an investigation) transfers the content of the activity to the mind of the student. (pp. 917–922)

As a result, teachers must be mindful of the assumptions placed on a student's learning and that routines are in place to test assumptions of where students are in their learning and then to act accordingly. Often as teachers, we don't know our students' interpretation of the information we or others are sharing with them and what decisions they are making as a result. In fact, we often take limited data from students or from a small sample size of students in the class and then make an assumption of student learning. This can have devastating results on student learning.

We need to find out what each learner is thinking during their activities and from that evidence make decisions on what the best steps are for their learning. As McLean Davies et al. (2013) states, "Assessment of student work as evidence of learning lies at the core . . . a key underlying principle being that with a data-driven, evidence based approach to teaching and learning, teachers can manipulate the learning environment and scaffold learning for every student, regardless of the student's development or intellectual capacity" (pp. 96–98).

As discussed in earlier chapters, the way we teach (instructional strategies), the way students engage in their learning (learning strategies), and the way we give and receive feedback (feedback strategies) have a higher chance of making an impact on learning when we provide those strategies at a student's level of learning (Hattie & Donoghue, 2016; Hattie & Timperley, 2007; Marzano, 2017). Hattie and Donoghue (2016) discussed how exploring errors and misconceptions has a far greater effect on learning when students already possess surface knowledge than when they are first learning the material (Hattie & Donoghue, 2016). In order to utilize the appropriate strategies for learning, teachers need to establish routines that illuminate student thinking and ensure students are aware of their own understanding (i.e., orientation) so that both teachers and students can utilize the right strategy for substantially impacting learning.

Establishing Routines

Teachers should consider establishing routines that focus on developing and enhancing student *expertise* and *efficacy*. Chapter 2 spoke extensively to the idea of efficacy-based strategies and routines that teachers may use to cultivate efficacy. Here we focus expertise-based routines and orientation-based routines to move learning forward including,

1. Integrating *orientation* routines in daily lessons: routines that support students in understanding content expectations, their current performance, and next steps to improve (see additional information on these strategies in Chapter 2).

2. Establishing *expertise-based* routines: routines that support students at each level of complexity (i.e., surface, deep, and transfer).

Orientation Routines

The routines below are centered on three key questions that enable students to develop a command over their learning (i.e., orientation). The following routines are suggested during lessons.

Question 1: Where am I going in my learning?

The best classroom routines evoke student awareness of the expectations of a daily lesson or the overall unit. In my own classroom experiences and as observed through extensive research, students

Figure 4.1   **Summary of Teacher Actions When Building Student Expertise**

Orientation Routines = Routines That Enable Students, Teachers, and Peers to Answer These Questions:
• Where am I going in my learning?
• Where am I now in my learning?
• What next step do I need to take to improve my learning?
Expertise-Based Learning Routines = Routines That Support Students in Meeting the Following:
• Surface expectations
• Deep expectations
• Transfer expectations

tend to focus their mind on the context of a unit or lesson and the activities or tasks that teachers are requiring rather than the content or learning expectations of the classroom. In *Rigorous PBL by Design* (2017), I discussed how a project that focused on reintroducing wolves into Yellowstone National Park would more than likely focus students on the wolves and the national park rather than the Next Generation Standards on changes of energy through disruptions in complex food webs. Moreover, time and time again, I have found that students were most concerned with the elements of the task, such as the number of slides in a PowerPoint and due dates rather than the central premise of their argument.

In this way, students can face "cognitive drift" and move away from what really matters. Moreover, they may not inherently recognize complexity of core expectations of the unit or lesson. By establishing routines that explicitly focus on learning intentions and success criteria, students can clearly point out the learning expectations of the unit or lesson and explicitly articulate the levels of complexity of unit and lesson expectations (see Figure 4.2). Moreover, these routines illuminate for teachers students' understanding of expectations, which allows teachers to adapt their instruction. Figure 4.2 illustrates a series of routines that supports students in answering the question: Where am I/we going?

Figure 4.2   *Where are we going?* Routines

Routine	Description
Success Criteria Mapping— Surface, Deep, and Transfer	• Provide students with a series of success criteria and ask them to place them under each complexity level (i.e., surface, deep, and transfer). • See vignette Success Criteria Mapping.
What Makes Good (WMG) Bingo	• Provide students with the success criteria and have them create a Bingo card with each success criteria (i.e., "What makes good?"). • Next, teachers should randomly choose a section of the Bingo card and randomly select students to define the criteria, offer an example, and offer a non-example.
Comparing Models of Performance	• Provide students with a series of examples that represent success at surface, deep, and transfer. • Have students compare the examples and evaluate which examples meet the success criteria at each level. • Next, provide students with an opportunity to offer feedback to make each example better. • This routine can be augmented by giving students several examples without providing the learning intention and success criteria. • Have students review the examples and determine the success criteria. • Then have students organize the success criteria into surface, deep, and transfer. • Next ask students to identify the goal/intention of the unit/lesson.
Creating a Story	Provide students with a series of prompts to communicate the learning expectations to others that are not in the classroom. For example • For us to learn in this class, we _____, _____, _____. • We often get stuck and go back to _____. • As a result of these actions, we _____.

(Continued)

Figure 4.2   (Continued)

Routine	Description
Accordion Method	• Students start out in small groups to review the success criteria. • They begin by identifying what criteria are clear to them and what criteria are unclear (or muddy). • Next, all students come together as a large class to review the learning intentions and success criteria with the teacher and ensure clarity. • Next students get back into small groups and analyze a piece of work and identify what success criteria have been met. • The class then comes back together to calibrate their evaluation. • The class then goes back out and identifies next steps they would provide to improve the work sample. • The class then comes back together to synthesize the suggestions from the smaller groups.
Red Light/Green Light	The following routine enables students to identify and clarify open vs. closed success criteria. • Students review two success models of work that the teacher deems as successful. Both models should illustrate open and closed success criteria. • Students create a t-chart, labelling one column "Red Light" and the other column "Green Light." • Students identify all of the open (Green Light) and closed success criteria (Red Light). • Students share their findings with the class to narrow down the success criteria for the unit/lesson. • The teacher asks students if any other green light options should be included. • The teacher asks students to identify next steps they should take to begin addressing the green and red light criteria.
Flashlight	• Students are tasked with creating a product without identified success criteria. • Students review products from others and begin making a list of what appears to be successful in the examples that have been drafted.

Routine	Description
	• Students are then given an exemplar to review. • In groups, students compare their examples and their lists of success with that of the exemplar. • Students then create a new draft of success criteria and share those criteria with the teacher. • The teacher then co-constructs the success criteria with students and shares the list.
Linking Learning Intentions and Success Criteria to Tasks	• Teachers give students a product of what they will be eventually creating. • The teacher asks students to identify what criteria are necessary to build such a product. • The teacher gives students a different product that requires the same success criteria (but doesn't show students the success criteria). • The students identify any new criteria that are necessary to build such a product.
Depth of Complexity Discussion	1. Provide students with a list of success criteria. 2. Next, have students mark which success criteria are surface, deep, and transfer. Alternative 1. Co-construct success criteria. 2. Have students mark which success criteria are surface, deep, and transfer.
Creating Clarity Collective Process	See detailed description below.

Question 2: Where am I now in my learning?

After students have demonstrated that they know where they are going in their learning, routines associated with Question 2 *Where am I now in my learning?* involve students and teachers checking for discrepancies between expectations of learning and current performance (see Figure 4.5). As discussed earlier, a student's understanding of a gap in performance is critical to their learning. The following routines aim at enabling this change.

Creating Clarity Collectively Process

Creating Clarity Collectively Process is a routine that supports students in answering the question *Where are we going?* by engaging learners in the formation and use of learning intentions and success criteria. This routine requires a series of steps that are shown below. In addition, I have included two examples of how the routine works in descriptive and narrative writing.

Figure 4.3   Six Steps for Creating Clarity Collectively

STEP 1: Students Brainstorm Criteria

STEP 2: Students Review Teacher Developed Criteria

STEP 3: Students and Teachers Review Exemplars to Refine List

STEP 4: Students and Teachers Organize List Into Leveled Success Criteria

STEP 5: Students and Teachers Evaluate Examples of Previous Work

STEP 6: Students and Teachers Use Criteria for Feedback and Monitoring Performance

CLARITY

	Descriptive Writing—First Grade	Narrative Writing—Eighth Grade
STEP 1 *Students brainstorm criteria.*	The teachers provide the students with the learning intention for the unit. Example LI: In this unit, learners will understand how to identify the main topic and retell important details of a text. Learners will write an informative/explanatory text on one topic with facts and closure. Next the teacher asks students to brainstorm what success looks like to meet the learning outcome. Example: The teacher asks the students to come up with what success would look like for a student to write an essay about something important to them (dog, family, vacation, etc.). The students then develop a list of potential criteria.	The teachers provide the students with the learning intention for the unit. Example LI: In this unit, learners will understand how to write narratives. Learners will understand how to determine theme or central ideas and their relationship to the text. Next the teacher asks students to brainstorm what success looks like to meet the learning outcome. Example: The teacher asks the students to think of a story from either a book, storyteller, movie, or podcast that was fantastic. Next, the teacher asks the students to brainstorm a list of what makes such stories successful. The students then develop a list of potential criteria.
STEP 2 *Students review teacher developed criteria.*	The teacher provides students with a list of teacher generated success criteria (see below for an example). Example: Teacher proposed success criteria	The teacher provides students with a list of teacher generated success criteria (see below for an example). Example: Teacher proposed success criteria

Surface	Deep	Transfer	Surface	Deep	Transfer
• I will use facts to tell about my topic. • I will use nouns, verbs, and adjectives in my writing. • I will identify the main topic of a text	• I will write different types of sentences that relate the main topic with details.	• I will write a text on one topic with supporting details to a main topic and conclusion.	• I will identify the techniques a writer uses to create a narrative. • I will describe the five elements of narrative: theme, characters, settings, plot, and point of view.	• I will analyze narrative techniques used by writers. • I will explain relationships between a theme and character, setting, plot, and point of view.	• Given any prompt, I will write a narrative piece about a real or imagined event appropriate to the task, audience, and purpose.

STEP 3 *Students and teachers review exemplars to refine success criteria list.*	Teachers provide students with several exemplars, including past student work and work from experts in the field. Teachers also ask students to consider adding potentially new success criteria.
STEP 4 *Students and teachers organize list into leveled success criteria.*	Teachers then provide students with the opportunity to sort the criteria into surface, deep, and transfer categories. Teachers may provide students with verbs that match each level to provide a scaffold in their learning.

(Continued)

(Continued)

	Descriptive Writing—First Grade	Narrative Writing—Eighth Grade
STEP 5 *Students and teachers evaluate examples of previous work.*	Next, teachers give students examples of students' previous work and have students assess the level of success for each example.	
STEP 6 *Students and teachers use success criteria for feedback and monitoring performance.*	Lastly, teachers ask students to use success criteria as they engage in their work and give feedback to others. Ask students to 1. Identify their own performance 2. Give and receive accurate feedback (aligned to success criteria and references examples) that moves the learning forward for all Teachers use a checklist (see below) to ensure that they have developed and formed with students quality learning intentions and success criteria.	

Figure 4.4   Creating Clarity Collectively Checklist

Learning Intentions

☐ The learning intentions state the goal of learning.

☐ The learning intentions are stated in student friendly language.

☐ The learning intentions use verbs at the highest complexity level for learning.

☐ The learning intentions are free of context.

Success Criteria

☐ The success criteria provide the ingredients for meeting the learning intention.

☐ The success criteria do not mention tasks and contexts.

☐ The success criteria are written at all levels of complexity (surface, deep, and transfer).

Engage in Learning Intentions and Success Criteria With Learners

☐ Students help draft and modify success criteria.

☐ Students use success criteria and exemplars to give and receive feedback.

☐ Students track individual and collective progress and proficiency via success criteria, exemplars, and assessment.

Figure 4.5   *Where am I now in my learning?* Routines

Routines	Description
Know/Need to Know (NTK)	• Students create a t-chart: The right column includes the title "Know" and the left column includes the title "Need to Know." • Individually, students should write down all of the information they already know based on the learning intentions and success criteria of the unit.

Routines	Description
	• Next, teachers ask them to pair share what they know related to the success criteria. During the pair share, the "listener" asks the "sharer" to provide examples and non-examples of what the student knows. The pair then switches roles and repeats the process.
	• Teachers then have each group share out their "know" list.
	• Teachers then have students draft "need to knows" related to success criteria.
Basketball	• Teachers announce to students that they will begin playing "basketball." The teacher will then review the rules.
	○ Any hands raised symbolize the need to ask a question not to answer questions.
	○ The teacher does not respond to statements made by students until at least five students have passed the question and response to each other.
	○ If you pass the question without responding, you will have a chance before the teacher responds to provide an answer.
	• The teacher then provides a question (Does global warming create a greater challenge to communities near forests?) or comment (Viruses are living.).
	• The teacher then states a student's name, and the student then provides a response (best if student selection is random). Once they respond, the question is passed to another student. This continues until at least five students have responded.
	• Next, the teacher asks all students to craft a response on their whiteboard (this could be offered via a multiple choice) and share with the rest of the class.
	• Next, the teacher will decide to (a) clarify, (b) provide feedback, and/or (c) continue playing basketball.
	• This routine works well with whiteboard conversations, structured inquiry, gallery walk, and mind the gap.
Whiteboard Conversations	• Students should draw two lines on their whiteboard so there are three columns.
	• Students create groups.
	• Students are then given a prompt.
	• Next, the students write down their individual responses on the whiteboard on the left column of the board.

(Continued)

Figure 4.5   (Continued)

Routines	Description
	• Then they discuss their thinking with the entire group. One way to discuss is to have each person share their responses one at a time. When that person shares, the other two students ask clarifying questions to ensure they fully understand what they heard. This is repeated two more times. • The students then create a mutual response to the prompt in the middle of the board. What is our collective response to the response? • Next, the teacher opens up a discussion or offers direction instruction to the students. They then discuss with their group the information they received and craft a new responses in the far right column. • The teacher then has them show their responses to the class. • The teacher then asks students to discuss the changes in the information from the first response to the last response.
Paint by Numbers	• Students are given another student's work (or a sample of previous work) and asked to identify success criteria at surface, deep, and transfer that have been met. • Students are then given their work back with the identifiers from another student. Students are then asked to review their work and identify what next steps they need to take.
A Through D	• Provide students with four flash cards (each with a letter A, B, C, and D). • Pose a question/comment to students with four options for answering the inquiry. • Have students meet with other students who selected similar options to identify why they selected that option. • Next share out. • Finally, provide the answer and have students discuss the differences between their answer and the answer presented.
D3: Daily Dissonance Discussions	• Begin the class by showing a video, sharing a story, or describing a personal narrative of being incorrect and having to engage in a "painful process" or "healthy level of stress" to correct the understanding or skill. • Next, present students with a position (All Republicans want to eliminate entitlements) or question (Is there more than one way to show how many 1/2s are in a 1/4?)? • Next, have students post their responses on a document and show it to others.

Routines	Description
	• Next provide students with information to support, refute, and correct their initial position.
	• Next have students share the discrepancy between previous understanding and new information.
	• Finally, have students present out in groups what they know now and have them explain how what they learned differs from their original thinking. Have students articulate how they handled the change in their learning.

Question 3: What next step do I need to take to improve my learning?

Routines must be established that best support students in their next steps in learning each day (see Figure 4.6). A few key ideas are recommended to consider when devising routines: First, students remember what they think about on a daily basis. One of the best ways to center students thinking on core academic content knowledge and skill is to have them focus on reading, writing, and talking. Second, certain strategies seem to have a higher probability of making an impact on student learning at varying levels of complexity (surface, deep, and transfer). In essence, our approaches should meet students where they are in their learning.

Figure 4.6   *What next steps do I need to take to improve my learning? Routines*

Routines	Description
Workshops: Surface, Deep, and Transfer	• Workshops are often 20–45 minutes in duration. Students may be structured in small groups (5–10 students) or engage as an entire class (20–34).
	• Workshops are structured as follows:
	Stage 1: Warm Up: Review success criteria, test student prior knowledge, and identify key areas of need (see Figure 4.7).
	Stage 2: Set: Engage in instruction at appropriate level of complexity—surface, deep, and transfer. Teachers provide opportunities for guided practice and independent practice.
	Stage 3: Cool Down: Review progress toward success criteria and discuss changes in student prior knowledge and identify key areas of need.

(Continued)

Figure 4.6   (Continued)

Routines	Description
Dialogue Centers	• Centers are a series of spaces set aside in a classroom that allow students to engage in learning content with a small group of students largely independent of direct teacher input. • Centers are structured as follows: Stage 1: Before students visit the centers, they review the learning intentions and success criteria and review their prior knowledge and the next steps they need to take in their learning. Stage 2: Students move to a center in small groups and begin engaging in the activity that is placed in front of them. In the last minute of the center, they summarize their learning and show their learning to the teacher via a whiteboard or device. Stage 3: Rotate and repeat Stage 2. Stage 4: Students synthesize their learning from each of the centers via a whole discussion or independent reflection. Stage 5: Students review their progress toward success criteria and discuss changes in their prior knowledge and identify key areas of need. • Centers are a critical routine for enabling students to transition across levels of complexity (e.g., surface to deep and deep to transfer).
Protocols for Progress	• Students use a series of procedures for discussing their progress with others and determining next steps in their learning. • The text and the appendix include a series of protocols that students may use to discuss and improve their learning, including, Resource 6.1 Critical Friends Protocol, Resource 6.2 What? So What? Now What? Protocol, Resource 6.5 Constructivist Tuning Protocol, and Resource 6.6 Learning Dilemma Protocol.
The Fundamentals	• Students establish clear learning goals that will support them in their learning as they review the learning intentions and success criteria. As students progress toward meeting the success criteria, teachers have them inspect their learning goals and identify what next steps they need to take to improve their learning as well as celebrate their successes. • The appendix includes an example of this routine and examples of learner reflections (see Figure 6.10a and Figure 6.10b).

Routines	Description
Check In—Room for Improvement (CIRFI) Protocol	• The CIRFI Protocol is a very powerful routine for supporting students who are high proficiency but low progress. • The protocol begins by having students identify their strongest work in class. • Next, the students identify where they are making progress and where they are still struggling in their learning. Students often review the success criteria at surface, deep, and transfer to make a determination of their performance. • Next, the students identify work habits that will support them in their learning, obstacles that are in their way (including personal habits), teacher support needs, and finally, exploring opportunities that may help them in their learning. • An example of the template is used in Figure 1.6.
Co-Construct Rubrics	• Build a one-point rubric with students to identify next steps in meeting outcomes (an example is provided in the Activities section of this chapter).
Lesson Freeze	• During student work time, state "freeze" and randomly assign a student to share their work with others. Have students provide feedback on strengths and potential next steps to improve learning.
I/We Have an Idea!	• Ask students to identify other ways to demonstrate their competency. Once they identified a new means for showcasing their learning, have them provide a rationale for why that process will better show their learning as opposed to what has been recommended by the teacher.

The Power of the 3 Essential Questions of Learning for Learners

Ninth-Grade Learner

Indianapolis, Indiana

As a learner, I have appreciated having a guide or map for my learning. Many times in my learning I have been confused on what has been expected of me, and I resorted to waiting for the teacher or my friend to tell me what I need to do. Or I would revert to focusing on completing the assignment or searching for tasks that I needed to do rather than really understanding and focusing on the actual things I needed to understand.

(Continued)

(Continued)

Over the past year, my teacher has established what she calls "routines" that have helped me focus on the 3 key questions. For example, our teacher will freeze our lessons and we all stop what we are doing and look at someone's work on the projector. We will review our learning intentions and success criteria and then give feedback to move their learning forward. This really helps the student getting the feedback and me in making sure my work is meeting the expectations of learning. In some ways, these routines are like a "learning tripwire," constantly refocusing us on what matters.

Expertise-Based Strategies

Student learning is improved when we align our teaching strategies to students' level of learning (surface, deep, and transfer). Before reviewing the routines, it is important to remember that each level of learning is of equal importance (see Figure 4.7). Moreover, there is no specific sequence that is required for students to develop an equal proportion of surface, deep, and transfer. There are multiple entry points for teachers to ensure an equal intensity of surface, deep, and transfer learning.

Our goal is to ensure students have an equal proportion of surface, deep, and transfer learning.

Figure 4.7   Relationship of Complexity Levels

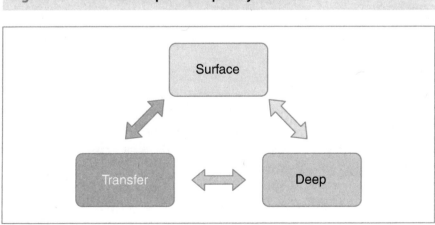

Figure 4.8 Three Pathways for Learning

Pathway 1 Problem–Project- Based Approach	Pathway 2 Traditional Sequencing	Pathway 3 Conceptual Entry
Transfer	1. Surface	1. Deep
Surface	2. Deep	2. Surface
Deep	3. Transfer	3. Transfer
Transfer		

Sequencing Developing Expertise Routines

When sequencing progress of learning routines for students, think about routines across a unit and routines within a lesson.

Implementing Routines Across a Unit

Pathway 1: Problem–Project-Based Approach

One way to support student learning is to provide the students with the transfer-level expectation at the beginning of the unit. This provides them with a clear sense of the rigorous expectations of the unit and enables students to see the rationale for learning surface and deep outcomes.

Pathway 1 (extensively discussed in *Rigorous PBL by Design*, McDowell, 2017) begins by launching students into a transfer-level situation (i.e., students are faced with an application-based scenario) on the first day of the unit. The students are then guided to identify what key success criteria at surface and deep are required to meet the transfer expectations. Once students have a clear sense of learning intentions and success criteria at all levels of complexity, the teacher then provides a sequence of lessons that typically start at surface and move toward deep and transfer over the duration of the unit. Figure 4.9 provides a simple visual to depict the sequence of learning across each level of complexity. Figure 4.10 provides a detailed scope and sequence of a problem–project-based learning experience for learners.

Figure 4.9   Pathway 1: Problem–Project-Based Approach

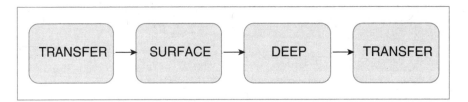

Figure 4.10   Suggested Scope and Sequence for Pathway 1: Problem–Project-Based Approach

Sequence	Description	Suggested Routines
Day 1–2	• Provide transfer expectations. • Unpack learning intentions and success criteria at surface and deep to meet transfer expectations. • Engage in pre-assessments to identify scope of student understanding relative to learning intentions and success criteria.	• Linkage • Red Light/Green Light • Know/NTK • Basketball
Day 3–7 (or more)	• Engage students in lessons to build their core competencies at surface and deep levels. • Engage students in a variety of experiences to discuss the following questions: *Where am I going in my learning? Where am I now? And What's next?*	• Lessons • Dialogue Centers (Figure 4.6) • Basketball
Day 8	• Engage in post-assessment (2/3rds the way through the unit) to identify student progress and proficiency and to devise next steps with learners.	• Paint by Numbers • Whiteboard Conversations
Day 9–11	• If necessary, engage students in lessons to build their core competencies at surface and deep levels. • Engage students in lessons related to transfer-level expectations.	• Lessons • Dialogue Centers (Figure 4.6) • Check-In/Room for Improvement Protocol (Figure 1.6)
Day 12–13	• Engage in transfer-level product presentations. • Reflections	• Protocols for Progress • The Fundamentals

Ray McClintok, Lead Teacher
School for Environmental Leadership
San Rafael, California

The ultimate outcome for kids in my class is for them to use content as a catalyst to formulate and support a claim. I want my students to be able to make an argument with logic and reason, and this requires students to understand a subject thoroughly. Facts precede skill, and yet both are important and both must be of value to a teacher. We can't sit at the content phase only, just building basic knowledge. I have to make sure we move to deep and transfer during a unit of instruction, and I need learners to see the importance of moving along these levels of complexity with me. Moreover, we can't just teach students critical thinking skills with limited core content. Or stated differently, students cannot just engage in transfer-level skills of applications of learning without surface knowledge. Both core content and critical thinking skills must be integrated.

To support students in developing surface, deep, and transfer learning, students are best served through problem- and project-based learning. Beginning the learning process with students at the transfer level and illuminating the expectations for high levels of learning and then scaffolding the core content and skills they need to learn to meet such expectations.

I have, however, made a few adjustments in how I apply the methodology to ensure high levels of learning. Firstly, I greatly value surface level (or core content knowledge) and need students to develop basic knowledge and skills before engaging in deeper learning. I need to use teaching approaches such as direct instruction during the first few days and then adjust my approach as we move to deep and transfer learning. Secondly, I don't spend a significant amount of time having students engage in and focus on long, drawn out tasks such as long papers or PowerPoints. Rather, I have students engage in shorter problems and tasks to focus their mental effort on learning. Rather than a 10-page paper, they engage in a 2- to 3-page paper with an oral presentation and a debate. This change in classroom practice moves students away from being bogged down in tasks and mentally focused on engaging in authentic problems and learning the necessary knowledge and skills.

Thirdly, I have students constantly "switch" or change their perspective when they are engaging in a project. For example, in one project I had 50% of my students spend 15 minutes developing arguments for the ban on the use of plastic straws and 50% of my students spend 15 minutes developing arguments against the ban on plastic straws. After 15 minutes, I have had

(Continued)

(Continued)

students switch their role and make the counterargument for 5 minutes. Students were able to draw on core content, engage in authentic collaboration with various students, and craft an argument that was incredibly powerful.

When done this way, a problem–project-based approach is an effective way to illustrate expectations, scaffold across levels of complexity, and then facilitate accordingly. I have never seen students so engaged when they began to focus less on tasks, shift to different perspectives, and take on new variables in a problem that was not there to begin with. As such, my learners have shown high levels of performance and engagement through learning.

To illustrate Pathway 1, the math example from the introduction (Figures 0.5 and 0.6) is revisited in Figure 4.11. In Pathway 1, the Problem–Project-Based Approach, teachers would present the transfer-level work on Day 1 (i.e., applying multiplication of fractions in different contexts, including finding out the car's rate in feet/hour and finding out the rate of a boat in ft/min when given yards/minute). Teachers would then assess student learning and go back and teach surface level (define multiplication of fractions and how to multiply fractions), then transition to deeper-level work (justify and estimate the products of two fractions), and then finally, go back to the transfer problems and answer them. The pacing is often adjusted based on the prior knowledge and rate of learning in the classroom.

Pathway 2: A Traditional Approach

One way to support student learning is to provide each student with clear expectations of initial surface-level expectations. This provides students with enough data to not exhaust working memory and allow them to focus on the learning expectations at hand. Once surface-level expectations are discussed, teachers would then engage students in learning such expectations using aligned instructional, feedback, and learning strategies at the surface level (see Figure 1.1). As learners begin developing surface-level expectations, teachers begin reviewing deep- and transfer-level success criteria and providing appropriate interventions.

Figure 4.11   Learning Intention and Success Criteria Revisited

Learning Intention: I will apply multiplication of fractions.		
Surface	**Deep**	**Transfer**
• Multiply fractions. • Define multiplication of fractions.	• Justify and estimate the products of two fractions.	• Apply multiplication of fractions in different contexts.
$7/8 \times 1/3 = 7/24$	(number line showing 0, 1/3, 2/3, 1 with $\frac{7}{?}$)	$\frac{10 \text{ yds}}{1 \text{ min}} \rightarrow \frac{\text{ft}}{\text{min}}$ $\frac{\text{yds}}{\text{min}} \cdot \boxed{\frac{\text{ft}}{\text{yds}}} = \frac{\text{ft}}{\text{min}}$ $\frac{10 \cancel{\text{yds}}}{1 \text{min}} \cdot \frac{3 \text{ft}}{1 \cancel{\text{yd}}} = \frac{10 \cdot 3 \text{ft}}{1 \text{min} \cdot 1} = \frac{30 \text{ft}}{1 \text{min}}$ What's the car's rate in feet/hour? $\text{Rate} = \frac{72 \text{mi}}{1 \text{hr}} \qquad 1 \text{mi} = 5280 \text{ft}$ $\boxed{\frac{5280 \text{ft}}{1 \text{mi}}} \text{ or } \frac{1 \text{mi}}{5280 \text{ft}} \qquad \frac{\cancel{\text{mi}}}{\text{hr}} \cdot \frac{\text{ft}}{\cancel{\text{mi}}} = \frac{\text{ft}}{\text{hr}}$ $\frac{72 \cancel{\text{mi}}}{1 \text{hr}} \cdot \frac{5280 \text{ft}}{1 \cancel{\text{mi}}} = \frac{72 \cdot 5280 \text{ft}}{1 \text{hr} \cdot 1}$ $= \boxed{380,160 \text{ft}}$

Figure 4.12   Pathway 2: A Traditional Approach to Learning

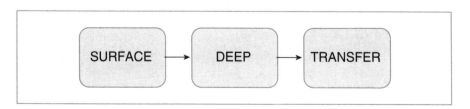

Pathway routines include the following:

Figure 4.13   Suggested Routines for Pathway 2: A Traditional Approach

Sequence	Description	Suggested Routines
Day 1–2	• Unpack learning intentions and success criteria at surface to meet deep and transfer expectations. • Engage in pre-assessments to identify scope of student understanding relative to learning intentions and success criteria.	• What Makes Good Bingo • Comparing Models of Performance
Day 3–7 (or more)	• Engage students in lessons to build their core competencies at surface and deep levels. • Engage students in a variety of experiences to discuss the following questions: *Where am I going in my learning? Where am I now? And What's next?*	• Dialogue Centers (Figure 4.6) • Lessons
Day 8	• Engage in post-assessment (2/3 of the way through the unit) to identify student progress and proficiency and to devise next steps with learners.	• Paint by Numbers • Whiteboard Conversations
Day 9–11	• If necessary, engage students in lessons to build their core competencies at surface and deep levels. • Engage students in lessons related to transfer-level expectations.	• Lessons • Dialogue Centers (Figure 4.6) • Check-In/Room for Improvement Protocol (Figure 1.6)
Day 12–13	• Engage in transfer-level product presentations. • Reflections	• Protocols for Progress • The Fundamentals

Unlike Pathway 1: the problem–project-based approach, teachers teaching the learning intentions and success criteria shown in Figure 4.12 would begin their instruction at the surface level (define multiplication of fractions and how multiply fractions), then transition to deeper level work (justify and estimate the products of two fractions), and then present the transfer-level work on the final few days of the unit (i.e., applying multiplication of fractions in different contexts, including finding out the car's rate in feet/hour and finding out the rate of a boat in ft/min when given yards/minute). The pacing is often adjusted based on the prior knowledge and rate of learning in the classroom.

Unlike Pathways 1 or Pathway 2, teachers using the conceptual entry would begin their instruction at the deeper-level work (justify and estimate the products of two fractions), then going to surface level (define multiplication of fractions and how to multiply fractions), then transitioning to the transfer-level work on the final few days of the unit (i.e., applying multiplication of fractions in different contexts, including finding out the car's rate in feet/hour and finding out the rate of a boat in ft/min when given yards/minute). The pacing is often adjusted based on the prior knowledge and rate of learning in the classroom.

Implementing Routines During Daily Lessons

Regardless of the pathway students are led down, a potential sequence for each lesson is shown in Figure 4.16. For instance, a teacher that selects the traditional, project- or problem-based, or conceptual entry would all engage in a fairly routine lesson sequence on a daily basis.

Figure 4.14   Pathway 3: Conceptual Entry Sequence

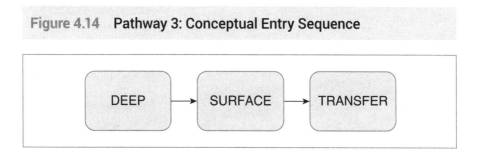

Figure 4.15   Suggested Routines for Pathway 3: Conceptual Entry Sequence

Sequence	Description	Suggested Routines
Day 1–2	• Unpack learning intentions and success criteria at surface and deep to meet transfer expectations. • Engage in pre-assessments to identify scope of student understanding relative to learning intentions and success criteria.	• WMG Bingo • Comparing Models of Performance

(Continued)

Figure 4.15   (Continued)

Sequence	Description	Suggested Routines
Day 3–7 (or more)	• Engage students in lessons to build their core competencies at surface and deep levels. • Engage students in a variety of experiences to discuss the following questions: *Where am I going in my learning? Where am I now? And What's next?*	• Dialogue Centers (Figure 4.6) • Lessons
Day 8	• Engage in post-assessment (2/3 of the way through the unit) to identify student progress and proficiency and to devise next steps with learners.	• Paint by Numbers • Whiteboard Conversations
Day 9–11	• If necessary, engage students in lessons to build their core competencies at surface and deep levels. • Engage students in lessons related to transfer-level expectations.	• Lessons • Dialogue Centers (Figure 4.6) • Check-In/Room for Improvement Protocol (Figure 1.6)
Day 12–13	• Engage in transfer-level product presentations. • Reflections	• Protocols for Progress • The Fundamentals

Figure 4.16   Potential Routines for Daily Lessons

Sequence	Description
BEGINNING (10–15 minutes)	• Teacher supports students in answering four investigative questions (Where am I going in my learning? Where am I now in my learning? What next step do I need to take to improve my learning? and, How do I improve my learning and that of others?). • Based on the orientation of the lesson in the unit or time of year, teachers may want to emphasize particular routines over others. For example, if the lesson is close to the beginning of the unit, the teacher may want to emphasize routines that ensure student clarity of expectations (e.g., Linkage or Flashlight).

Sequence	Description
MIDDLE (15–30 minutes)	• Teachers provide lessons at surface, deep, and transfer to enable students to move forward in their learning.
	• Recommended routines for checking student understanding include Whiteboard Conversations, Basketball, Paint by Numbers.
	• Based on student responses and performance, teachers engage in specific targeted instruction.
CONCLUSION (5–10 minutes)	• Teacher supports students in reflecting on their progress related to the four investigative questions (Where am I going in my learning? Where am I now in my learning? What next step do I need to take to improve my learning? and, How do I improve my learning and that of others?).
	• Recommended routines include CIRFI, The Fundamentals, Protocols for Progress, and Know/Need to Know.

When implementing units and lessons, it is paramount to provide routines that center on students' cognitive needs at surface, deep, and transfer. As discussed in previous chapters, students need different instructional, learning, and feedback strategies at surface, deep, and transfer. The following subsections offer a few routines that may assist learners in their learning.

Teaching to Surface Routines

Surface routines are designed to support students in understanding ideas and/or developing skills. At this level, students are working to define, label, and list ideas and practice implementing a skill. The following routines are samples of what educators could use to support this level of learning for students. These routines incorporate instructional, feedback, and learning strategies that are aligned with the "best fit" strategies discussed in Chapter 1 (See Figure 1.1).

Teaching to Deep Routines

Deep routines are designed to support students in relating ideas and/or developing skills. At this level, they are attempting to compare and contrast ideas and skills. The following routines are samples of what educators could use to support this level of learning for students.

Figure 4.17   Teaching to Surface Sample Routines

Routines	Description	Examples
Mind the Gap	Students are tasked with comparing and contrasting their previous/current understanding to new information shared with them from peers, educators, and resources.	Students create a three-column table on a piece of paper and write down their current thinking, others' thinking, and changes in their learning. (left side—current, middle—new, right column—changes in their learning).
Surveying the Scene	Students are tasked with learning several new terms in a new discipline and work to develop an advanced organizer to support their learning.	Students are provided with a variety of resources and tasked with creating an outline or graphic organizer with the key facts/ideas related to the learning intention. Students are provided with a model of an advanced organizer to support their learning.
Gumshoe	Students are given progressively less information on worked examples to enable them to eventually solve the problems.	Students are given several worked examples of problems that gradually illustrate less and less information over time. Students are then tasked with completing those problems and discussing what is required in solving problems.

Figure 4.18   Routines for Deep Learning

Routine	Description	Examples
Jigsaw +	Students are charged with engaging in a jigsaw and then creating a product for showcasing their understanding.	• Students are assigned to groups of 3–5 and are tasked with selecting each group member to become an expert on an idea or skill. • Students then go to "expert" groups to understand that idea. • Students then go back to their original group and share their findings. • The entire group then develops a Venn diagram to show their understanding of the relationships between ideas. • The group then receives feedback from others and evaluates their understanding with others.

Routine	Description	Examples
Connect 4	• Students are charged with creating a concept map to share relationships among ideas.	• Version A: Students connect 4 ideas together by showing a dotted line for indirect relationships, no line for no relationship, and a non-dotted line for a direct relationship. • Version B: Students connect an idea by showing it in four different ways (A: visual, B: story, C: a worked problem, and D: contexts related to the situation).
Linked Learning	• Students are tasked with sharing their understanding among ideas with others at the classroom or group level. Students are tasked with linking ideas to opinions.	• Students share their understanding of principles of a discipline. • Students then share ways in which these principles play in the "real world" (i.e., political, social, economic). • Students then form into groups to debate/discuss their opinions in relation to these principles and opinions.

Knowing Levels of Complexity

Seventh-Grade Learner

Phoenix, Arizona

I was introduced to surface, deep, and transfer at the beginning of the school year, and I thought this idea was really helpful. As a student, I don't always know what to do first and what's harder to begin with in my learning. When our teacher introduced these ideas to the class, I thought it was incredibly beneficial to sequence my thinking of what and when I needed to learn content, but it also allowed me to think about what I do when I'm first learning something, what I do when I'm at the deep level, and what I do when I'm at transfer. Our teacher helps us experience these levels of learning by sharing success criteria with important verbs and going through routines that help us with each level. I found this to not only help me in being clear and getting better in my own learning but also to understand why decisions are being made for why I'm doing certain activities or tasks.

Teaching to Transfer Routines

Transfer relates to a student's ability to apply their understanding of core academic content and skills to different contexts. As Jay McTighe (2018) argues, "Transfer goals . . . specify what we want students to be able to do with learning in the long run when confronted by new opportunities and challenges" (pp. 15–16). For example, let's say we have a student who can calculate a percentage (surface) and understands that a percentage is breaking a number into one hundred equal parts (deep) and now needs to be able to apply that understanding to a number of situations including

- The % of people who voted for gender-neutral toys

- The % drop in total honeybee numbers

- The % increase in currency inflation

Humans inherently struggle with identifying the underlying core content from a situation, and therefore, teachers must support students in developing the ability to transfer their content knowledge across contexts. In *Rigorous PBL by Design* (McDowell, 2017), teachers designed projects and problems that ensured students were able to

Figure 4.19   General Routines for Transfer Learning

	Description	Examples
Sherlock or Show Me the Evidence	Students determine similarities and differences between problems by using accurate evidence.	Students offer conclusions based in research-based evidence.
Ambidextrous Learning	Students address complex problems and issues in and across contexts by using divergent and convergent thinking.	Students establish an agreed upon problem-solving model and use focus (convergent—using real-world limitations or constraints) and flare (divergent—not using real-world limitations or constraints) to solve problems.
Relational Roulette	Students discern patterns and themes in core academics and within and across contexts.	Students use logic models, flow charts, and graphic organizers to depict similarities and differences between variables in different situations.

mentally separate the core academic content from the context of the project. The shown in Figure 4.19 routines provide students with support on transferring their learning.

Conclusion

By continually engaging in efficacy and expertise-based routines, teachers and students will be able to more accurately understand performance and more effectively intervene to promote student learning toward identified learning goals. Efficacy-based routines focus on supporting teachers and students in clarifying expectations, student performance, and identifying next steps. Expertise-based routines focus on aligning instructional strategies to levels of complexity. These routines can be sequenced in a variety of ways to support students in meeting surface, deep, and transfer expectations. In the next chapter, we take a deep dive into transfer and ensuring that high proficiency is also high progress.

REFLECTION QUESTIONS

- What stands out for you in this chapter regarding integrating routines for efficacy and expertise?

- Which sequence of progress for learning routines resonates with you and your practice? Why?

- What systems do you have in place right now to check your assumptions and that of your students on their learning?

- How will you apply transfer routines in your classroom? When will you apply these routines?

ACTIVITIES

ACTIVITY 4.1

Step 1: Select an efficacy and expertise routine.

Step 2: Implement both routines over the two weeks.

You may want to ask a fellow teacher to observe or film you and the students going through the routine to support you in refining your practice (see Resource 6.11 Video Reflection Protocol).

Step 3: At the end of two weeks, engage in a feedback protocol with students on their perception of the new routines (see Resource 6.1 Critical Friends Protocol or Resource 6.5 Constructivist Tuning Protocol).

- -

ACTIVITY 4.2

Step 1: As a department, have each teacher select and implement a transfer level routine in the classroom.

Step 2: Once implemented, discuss collectively how such activities compare and contrast to previous routines in the classroom.

Step 3: Discuss next steps.

- -

ACTIVITY 4.3

After reviewing the scenarios presented in Figure 4.20, determine potential next steps in your planning to enhance student learning.

Figure 4.20   Teaching Scenarios

Scenarios	Description	Strategy	Next Steps
Adjustments	The learning process is mostly hidden from us, and we need to unmask the learning and respond.	(Efficacy-Based) Implement routines that enable students to answer efficacy based questions.	•

Scenarios	Description	Strategy	Next Steps
Alignment	Certain strategies have a higher probability of enhancing learning at different levels of learning.	(Expertise-Based) Align teaching and learning strategies to depth of complexity.	•
Inspect	We tend to make assumptions from our experiences and need to inspect whether those assumptions are true.	Continually check for understanding of our own impact, and take action.	•

Figure 4.21   **Learning Goals and Success Criteria at Levels of Complexity**

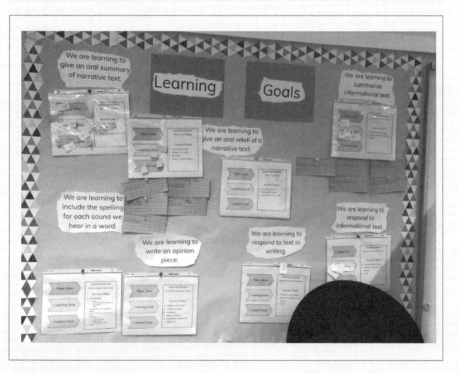

Source: Ross School; Ross, CA. Used with Permission.

ACTIVITY 4.4

Step 1: Ask colleagues to go back and review their individual responses in Activity 3.4, *Inspecting Leveled Success Criteria.* Specifically, have the team review these questions:

- How will you actively involve students in understanding and using the success criteria in their learning? How will you support each learner in providing self and peer feedback toward meeting the established leveled success criteria?

Step 2: Ask the team to consider how their answers have changed or stayed the same from their response in Chapter 3?

Step 3: Answer the following questions:

- How will you/we expose students to examples of excellence at surface, deep, and transfer?

- How will you/we provide students with the necessary vocabulary (i.e., success criteria) to discuss and provide feedback on pieces of work?

- How will you ensure students are engaged in giving and receiving accurate feedback to one another?

- How will you ensure students reflect on their work and reflect on their progress over time?

Step 4: As a team, reflect on how staff build each other's capacity to provide the necessary guidance to support learners in developing their expertise and efficacy.

- -

ACTIVITY 4.5
CREATING CLARITY TOGETHER

In this activity, teachers work with each other to identify strategies that actively involve students in the construction of and use of learning intentions and success criteria with others.

Step 1: As a team, ask colleagues to come up with the solutions to the following prompts:

1. How do we engage students in understanding and actively using learning intentions and success criteria? How do we ensure that

students are part of co-constructing success criteria with peers and teachers?

2. How do we ensure students are giving and receiving targeted feedback based on the learning intentions?

3. How do we use learning intentions and success criteria for students to track their own learning?

4. How can we inspect and improve our practice in regards to Questions #1 through 3 above?

NEXT STEPS

- In the next week of school, ask students the questions associated with orientation (e.g., *Where are we going in our learning? Where am I now in my learning?* and, *What's your next step?*). In light of the students' responses, select one strategy to implement with students. Next, identify what you expect students will say or do in the next few weeks. How do you expect this to change in one week? Three weeks? A grading term?

- Write down two assumptions you have right now regarding your students' awareness of their learning and their current performance. How will you check your assumptions? How will you share this information with students? What assumptions do they have?

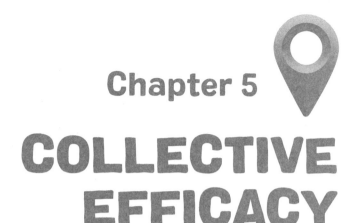

Chapter 5

COLLECTIVE EFFICACY

Developing Efficacy and Expertise as Professionals

We often think we associate understanding with abstraction. It's just the opposite.

—Moyers and Ganz (2013)

In the fall of 2015, I invited learners to observe a staff meeting and give us feedback on our performance in collaborating with one another. The learners were shocked to see that educators were engaging in many of the same behaviors and processes that they were applying in the classroom. One of the learners said to the staff, "You learn too! I thought you did all of these things in the classroom for us to learn. I never thought that you in fact did what we did to learn. You are shooting for +1 in your learning . . ." This chapter is all about putting into practice many of the strategies discussed in Chapters 1 through 4 to have a substantial impact on your learning and that of your colleagues.

The influence of collective teacher efficacy—that is, teachers working together to get better at impacting student learning, is found to be among the greatest influences in education (Hattie, 2009; Hattie & Donoghue, 2016; Dewitt, 2017). Simultaneously, collective efficacy can, at times, be a difficult idea to incorporate into practice. Rick Dufour and Robert Marzano (2011) have certainly brought the notion down to a concrete level by focusing on teacher teams via Professional Learning Community, whereby teachers, in teams, collectively utilize data to make changes in instruction and ultimately drive improvements in student achievement. Though certainly the intent of this process—the development of efficacious behaviors both personally as a teacher and collectively as a team, modeling such efficacious behaviors with students, focusing on growth data across levels of complexity (i.e., surface, deep, and transfer), and the idea of continuous learning—has taken a secondary focus to the process of reviewing proficiency data to make instructional decisions collectively. In this chapter, we will focus on developing individual and collective teacher efficacy and expertise through the focus of developing student efficacy and expertise over time.

Building Collective Efficacy

Brad Sever, Assistant Principal
Carmel High School
Carmel, Indiana

Someone who is high in efficacy is one who sets a goal and believes he or she can accomplish that goal. A rough day in the classroom can discourage even those teachers who have a high efficacy. It is imperative that structures are established to build teacher efficacy. After all, how do we expect to build student efficacy, unless we have teachers and administrators who can model the behavior they hope to see in students?

In the four years since we have focused on collective efficacy and ensuring the right beliefs and behaviors at Carmel High School, we have seen a growth in the amount of times teachers are utilizing coaching and collaboration. We have seen the number of co-plans increase from 215 the first year to 449 in the fourth year. We have also seen the number of peer coaching conversations go from 34 to 109. Our coaching conversations, [which] center around quality student work [and] co-planning with an individual teacher or with a group of teachers who teach the same course, have substantially increased. These are just a few examples of targeted ways collective efficacy is cultivated and nurtured.

Linking Professional and Student Efficacy

One way to provide a simplified view of teacher individual collective efficacy is to illustrate the relationship between teacher and students efficacy. Similar to student efficacy (see Chapter 2), teachers and teacher teams should focus on the three key elements of efficacy (orientation, activation, and collaboration) and use the same types of questions to improve overall learning (see via Figures 5.1 for questions associated with individual efficacy and 5.2 for collective efficacy-based questions).

Figure 5.1   Individual Student Efficacy and Teacher Individual Efficacy

	Individual Student Efficacy	Individual Teacher Efficacy
Orientation	Description • Where am I going in my learning? • Where am I now? • What's next?	Description • Where am I expecting learners to go in their learning? • Where are they now in their learning (surface, deep, and transfer) and their development of efficacious behaviors (orientation, activation, and collaboration)? • In light of the evidence, what impact am I having on learners? What next steps do I take to improve their learning? What did I learn through this process?
Activation	• What enables learners to persevere? • How do I learn? • What enables learners to recognize their successes and challenges? • What helps learners stay focused? • What strategies do I use when I'm bored? • What strategies have supported me in the past to learn content at surface, deep, and transfer?	• How do I persevere in my work as an educator? • How do I learn? • What enables me as a leader of learners to recognize my own successes and challenges in teaching? • What supports me in staying focused on substantially enhancing student learning in the areas of progress and proficiency? • What strategies do I use when I'm bored or become unmotivated? How do I face setbacks when my work does not meet my expectations or those of my team?

(Continued)

Figure 5.1   **(Continued)**

	Individual Student Efficacy	Individual Teacher Efficacy
	• What strategies do I use when I disagree, or I feel indifferent? • What strategies do I use when I'm confused? • What do I do when I don't know what to do? • What strategies do I use to continue to push my own learning?	• What strategies do I use to enhance my learning at surface, deep, and transfer? • What strategies do I use to share my disagreements? What strategies do I use when I feel indifferent? • What strategies do I use when I'm confused? • What do I do when I don't know what to do? • What strategies do I use to continually push my own thinking?
Collaboration	• How can others push my thinking? • What feedback can I seek to improve my learning? • How can others strengthen or challenge my ideas? • How do I pull someone's learning forward? • How do we collectively press forward and co-create a better solution together? • How do we "stay soft on people and hard on content" when discussing someone's work or reviewing data?	• How can others push my thinking? • What feedback can I seek to improve my learning? • How can others strengthen or challenge my ideas? • How do I pull someone's learning forward? • How do I support the team in collectively pressing forward with our work and co-creating a better solution together? • How do I "stay soft on people and hard on content" when discussing someone work or reviewing data?

Figure 5.2   **Collective Student Efficacy and Collective Teacher Efficacy**

	Collective Student Efficacy	Collective Teacher Efficacy
Orientation	Description • Where are we going in my learning?	Description • Where are we expecting learners to go in their learning?

	Collective Student Efficacy	Collective Teacher Efficacy
	• Where are we now? • What's next for the team?	• Where are our learners now in their learning (surface, deep, and transfer) and their development of efficacious behaviors (orientation, activation, and collaboration)? • In light of the evidence, what impact are we having on learners? What next steps do we need to take to improve their learning? What did we learn through this process?
Activation	• How do we persevere in our collective work? • How do we learn together? • What enables us to recognize our successes and challenges? • What helps us as a team stay focused? • What strategies do we use when we're bored? • What strategies have supported me in the past to learn content at surface, deep, and transfer? • What strategies do I use when I disagree or I feel indifferent? • What strategies do we use when we're confused? • What do we do when we don't know what to do? • What strategies do we use to continue to push our own learning?	• How do we persevere in our collective work? • How do we learn together and support each individual in their learning? • What enables us as a leader of learners to recognize our individual and collective successes and challenges in teaching? • What supports our team in staying focused on substantially enhancing student learning in the areas of progress and proficiency? • What strategies do we use when we are bored or become unmotivated? How do we face setbacks when our work does not meet our expectations? • What strategies do we use to enhance our learning at surface, deep, and transfer? • What strategies do we use to share our disagreements and continue listen to others? What strategies do we use when we feel indifferent? • What strategies do we use when members of the team are confused?

(Continued)

Figure 5.2   (Continued)

	Collective Student Efficacy	Collective Teacher Efficacy
		• What do we do when we don't know what to do? • What strategies do we use to continually push our thinking?
Collaboration	• How can others push our thinking? • What feedback can we seek to improve our learning? • How can others strengthen or challenge our ideas? • How do we pull someone's learning forward? • How do we collectively press forward and co-create a better solution together? • How do we "stay soft on people and hard on content" when discussing someone work or reviewing data?	• How can others push our thinking? • What feedback can we seek to improve our learning? • How can others strengthen or challenge our ideas? • How do we pull someone's learning forward? • How do we support the team in collectively pressing forward with our work and co-creating a better solution together? • How do we "stay soft on people and hard on content" when discussing someone's work or reviewing data?

As individual teachers and teacher teams begin focusing on efficacious behaviors, they should consider a progression of development. Similar to the progression explored for learners in Chapter 2, a three-phase progression is shown here whereby there is an introductory phase of learning efficacious strategies (Introducing Efficacious Behaviors), developing competency phase (Applying Efficacious Behaviors), and a phase of refinement (Reinforcing Efficacious Behaviors).

Individual and collective efficacy are enhanced when teachers and teacher teams engage in the following three steps:

- Design core tasks for professionals to impact learning

- Create a process for collective learning through teaming

- Structure the methods for determining, discussing, debating, and designing next steps for improvement.

Figure 5.3 Individual and Collective Teacher Efficacy Progression

	Orientation	Activation	Collaboration
Introducing Teacher Efficacy—Teachers and teacher teams are spending significant time providing background information on the need for efficacious behaviors and are trying different strategies that they may use consistently in the future.	• Teachers and teacher teams are unclear on the goals for impacting learning, the expectations of meeting stated goals of learning, and next steps related to improving the learning of children through their teaching. • Teachers are unclear on levels of learning and how to use various strategies to move learners through each level of complexity. • Teacher reflections are often focused on learner proficiency, unit/lesson design, student comportment, and meeting task deadlines as opposed to student progress across levels of complexity and students' engagement in the process of developing their own efficacy.	• Teachers and teacher teams are unclear on strategies that would support them in learning when they are stuck, bored, or indifferent. • Teachers and teacher teams are uncomfortable discussing their performance. • Teachers often associate the best teachers as those who have students with high proficiency levels or a higher number of years teaching.	• Teachers are inconsistent or inaccurate with giving and receiving feedback related to student expertise and efficacy results. • Teachers are uncomfortable sharing their work and receiving feedback. • Teachers often disengage in dialogue when solving collective problems where opinions vary.
Applying Individual Teacher Efficacious Behaviors—Individual and collective routines to discuss student performance relative to	• Teachers and teacher teams have established goals and means for data collection and struggle with developing a plan for determining next steps in improving learning for children.	• Teachers and teacher teams have attempted strategies that would support them in learning when they are stuck, bored, or indifferent.	• When prompted and scaffolded, teachers and teacher teams are giving and receiving accurate feedback.

(Continued)

Figure 5.3 (Continued)

	Orientation	Activation	Collaboration
teachers' impact on student learning begins to emerge during preparation time and common planning.	• Teachers have a clear sense of their proficiency and growth in meeting learning goals while failing to relate that learning to levels of complexity.	• Teachers and teacher teams are comfortable discussing their performance and have an openness to discussing their work in public. • Teachers and teacher teams often associate the best learners as those who are making changes to improve their own learning.	• Teachers state they are comfortable in giving and receiving feedback. • When prompted and scaffolded, teachers engage in dialogue to solve problems.
Reinforcing Individual Teacher Efficacious Behaviors Individual and collective routines to discuss teachers' impact on student learning are commonplace between and among teachers.	• Teachers are individually and collectively inspecting their impact, discussing plans of action, and sharing their results. • Teachers are questioning their prior knowledge and reflecting on steps they can take to improve upon their current understanding.	• Teachers and teacher teams are utilizing strategies that enable themselves to persevere when they are bored, stuck, or indifferent of the work. • Teachers and teacher teams are reflecting and planning for how to transfer such skills to other parts of their life.	• Teachers and teacher teams are giving and receiving accurate feedback to others. • Teachers are solving complex problems by integrating the ideas of others and testing assumptions. • Teachers use agreements, protocols, and norms to maintain relationships and solve problems.

Designing Core Tasks for Professionals to Impact Learning

Developing individual and collective teacher efficacy centers around the individual's and the group's ability to know the expectations of their core work which includes the following:

- Learners are gaining more than one year's growth in one year's time along learning intentions and success criteria at surface, deep, and transfer.

- Learners are developing efficacy by cultivating knowledge and skills in the areas of orientation, activation, and collaboration.

Firstly, educators must create standards for progress and proficiency in the area of expertise and efficacy. Secondly, teachers must collectively identify ways to determine progress and proficiency in the areas of efficacy and expertise. Finally, teachers must identify resources that will support them in making evidence-informed decisions. This aspect of articulating the core work of educators is critical, as it provides the information necessary for educators to determine their impact on learning and then identify corresponding actions to improve.

Establishing Standards for Developing Expertise and Efficacy

Teachers must establish a standard of academic proficiency and progress for the learners in their school. One way to begin this work is to establish levels of proficiency based on the continuum of complexity (i.e., surface, deep, and transfer) related to identified learning intentions. If those levels of complexity were established, then surface-level work or surface-level work with support from teachers would be "below proficiency," and deep- and transfer-level work would be categorized as "above proficiency" (McDowell, 2018). Secondly, teachers want to look at standardized approaches to determine the amount of progress students have made over a given period of time. In *The Lead Learner* (McDowell, 2018), the recommendation was to use effect sizes to identify student progress. (Several other approaches to measuring progress are discussed in the following subsection.)

Once established, teachers are able to measure both the rate of progress and the level of proficiency (surface, deep, and transfer) of each learner (see Figure 5.4 for an example). Figure 5.4 illustrates the use of an effect size on the horizontal axis to indicate growth over time. Moreover, Figure 5.4 (Resource 6.13b) shows surface, deep, and transfer levels to indicate the varying complexity levels within the area of proficiency. To see an example of a students' reference guide (visual cue) for this matrix, revisit Figure 2.1.

> *Figure 5.4 illustrates potential progress and proficiency scenarios that teachers will face in their classrooms or when looking at multiple classrooms. Students in Quadrant 1 will be showing high levels of progress and low levels of proficiency and as such are being substantially impacted by the teaching in the classroom. Students in Quadrant 2 will be showing high levels of progress but low levels of proficiency and as such are being substantially impacted by the teaching in the classroom. Students in Quadrant 3 are showing low levels of progress and high proficiency and as such are showing less than ideal growth by the teaching in the classroom. Finally, Quadrant 4 illustrates students that are showing low levels of progress and proficiency and as such are showing less than ideal growth and proficiency due to the teaching in the classroom.*

Teachers must also establish a standard for proficiency and progress of efficacy. As discussed in Chapter 2, proficiency may be viewed along a continuum of three key phases (Introducing Efficacious

Figure 5.4   Progress and Proficiency Matrix

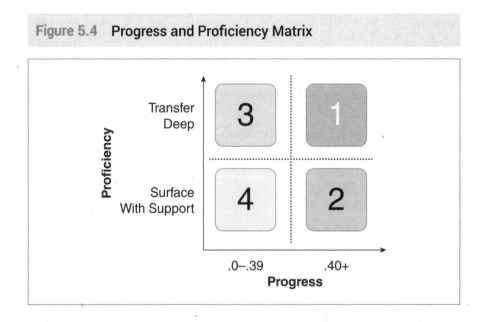

Behaviors, Applying Efficacious Behaviors, and Reinforcing Efficacious Behaviors). Each phase has a set number of success criteria that identify key expectations of learning for students.

To establish a standard of progression for efficacy, teachers should agree on expected growth of student learning within and across the three efficacy-based phases. From here, teachers may collect evidence of student individual and collective efficacy at the beginning of the school year and then identify select times throughout the year to collect, discuss, and take action on student efficacy data (see Resource 6.13a). As Hattie (2015) argues, evaluations of progress and proficiency data should be considered every 10 to 12 weeks to discourage overassessment while balancing the need for having the opportunity to take action.

Creating Tools to Measure Progress and Proficiency of Student Expertise and Efficacy

To engage in 10- to 12-week assessment cycles of student expertise and efficacy, teachers should consider the best means for determining student progress and proficiency. As mentioned above, one way to engage in this work is to use an effect size of .40, as this robust metric denotes one year's growth in one year's time (Hattie, 2012). Other recommendations include utilizing knowledge gain scores, which require teachers to establish point scheme (e.g., a four-point rubric) that are directly related to each level of complexity. This approach requires that teams agree on the level of growth that is deemed to be an adequate level of progress over the course of one year (Marzano & Waters, 2009). For example, in *Rigorous PBL by Design* (McDowell, 2017) a four-point scale was utilized to denote one score for each level of complexity—surface, deep, and transfer (see Figure 5.5). Imagine that a team decided that a 1.0 knowledge gain over a set of 10 to 12 weeks would be approximate to showing the appropriate progress toward one-year's growth. This would give the team the ability to then standardize their discussions on progress using knowledge gain scores.

Other approaches include incorporating expectation-setting sessions with teachers as they work together to identify anchor exemplars of student work at surface, deep, and transfer for a few key outcomes within three months (quarter school year), six months (semester), and nine to ten months (full school year). As Hattie (2015) argues,

> [T]eachers could be asked to bring two anonymous pieces of student work showing growth over three-plus months. They would then be asked to place the work along a curriculum-year line and have a robust discussion about progression based on

Figure 5.5   Four-Point Scale Linked to Levels of Complexity

Success Criteria	Score	
Transfer *Applying Understanding*	4.0	• Met transfer expectations
	3.5	• Partially met transfer expectations
Deep *Making Meaning*	3.0	• Met deep expectations
	2.5	• Partially met deep expectations
Surface *Building Knowledge*	2.0	• Met surface expectations
	1.5	• Partial success with surface expectations
With Support	1.0	• With instructional support, student met surface and deep
	0.5	• With instructional support, student met surface-level expectations
	0.0	• With instructional support, student has not met surface-level expectations

Source: Adapted from McDowell, 2017.

the teachers' judgements of growth and whether this progress is sufficient. This can lead to healthy debates about "what is means to be at__" and the development of a common conception of progress among teachers. (p. 7)

Imagine teachers from different grade levels in mathematics or English language arts coming together and reviewing student work at surface, deep, and transfer level at the beginning, middle, and end of each year and establishing expectations for those times of the school year. This would give teachers a common set of expectations of proficiency and progress over multiple years for learners. From this discussion, teachers could bring a sampling of current student work and discuss rates of progress and proficiency.

Beyond effect sizes, knowledge gain scores, and anchor papers, teachers may also use interviews, observations, and student-generated assessments to determine growth and proficiency (Marzano, 2009, 2010).

A team of teachers could interview a sampling of students on a series of questions that related to surface, deep, and transfer expectations at the beginning of a unit of instruction and then several weeks later and determine the rate of growth of students over time. Teachers may simply observe students as they engage in independent work, collaborative discussions, or project work and capture evidence of student performance and relative growth over time (see Resources 6.13d and 6.13e for discussion prompts and an example of data collection). Finally, students may request ways to show their evidence of learning over time that illustrates progress and proficiency.

As shown in Figure 5.6, many of these same tools may be used to collect evidence of student progress and proficiency toward developing efficacy. At Ross School in Northern California, select questions from the Learning Rounds template (see Figure 0.8) are used to create surveys, focus groups, and interviews (see appendix for examples, including Resources 6.12a to 6.12e). Teachers may also engage in observing students' action and listening to their language to get a sense of efficacious behaviors (see Resource 6.13a). Teachers can assess student expertise through classroom discussions (see Resource 6.12d). Finally, students may request ways to show their evidence developing efficacious behaviors, both at an individual level and in collaborative-based situations (such as working in a team).

As shown, there is no one way to measure student proficiency and progress, and in fact, the best means to measure one year's growth for learners is an important and ongoing discussion within a department and school. The key is for the discussion with the department or the school to have clear expectations of levels of complexity, standards of progress, and standards of proficiency and agreed upon tools to collect and discuss data. This will then drive the team to determine their performance and develop subsequent actions to improve.

Creating Resources for Determining Next Steps

The previous two steps allow teams to articulate where they are going (i.e., establishing standards for identifying proficiency and progress of expertise and efficacy) and means to identify where learners are currently in meeting these standards (i.e., identify tools for measuring proficiency and progress). In order to engage in analyzing a teacher's or team's impact on student learning via data and in determining next steps, teachers and teacher teams may need resources to assist in making informed instructional decisions. One suggestion is to develop a Best Fit Impact Model for learning (BFIM).

Figure 5.6   Potential Means for Capturing Progress and Proficiency in Developing Expertise and Efficacy

Developing Expertise	Developing Efficacy
Effect size—using pre- and post-assessment data to analyze proficiency and progress set against the .40 effect size. (Hattie, 2011)	Learning rounds—capturing student responses to questions during class time linked to orientation, activation, and collaboration before, during, and after the school year to measure progress and proficiency related to the development of efficacy. (McDowell, 2018)
Knowledge gain—establishing a set scale for levels of complexity, teachers analyze the amount of growth for students in their learning. (Marzano & Waters, 2009)	Survey data—conducting pre-/post-surveys with students on a series of questions that are aligned to orientation, activation, and collaboration. (McDowell, 2018)
Standardized benchmarking—utilizing a standardized assessment throughout the year to track growth, such as the Northwest Education Association Measure of Academic Performance. (e.g., Rasch Unit or RIT scores)	Focus groups—using similar questions to those of the learning rounds and survey data, teachers interview a few students to get a sense of their progress and proficiency related to efficacious behaviors.
Anchor work—comparing student work over time to exemplar work at surface, deep, and transfer. (Hattie, 2015)	Interviews—using similar questions to those posed on pre-post assessments, teachers interview students 1:1. These interviews often ask clarifying questions to get an in-depth understanding of the use of efficacious behaviors.
Interviews—using similar questions to those posed on pre-post assessments, teachers interview students 1:1. These interviews often ask clarifying questions to get an in-depth understanding of expertise. (Marzano, 2009)	Unobtrusive assessments—through observations before, during, and after class, teachers mark down changes in the use of efficacious behaviors in the classroom.
Student-generated assessments—students create their own approaches to demonstrating their progress and proficiency over time. (Marzano, 2009)	Unobtrusive assessments—through observations before, during, and after class, teachers mark down changes in the use of efficacious behaviors in the classroom.
Discussion—using prompts at surface, deep, and transfer, teachers can track student progress toward learning intentions and success criteria.	Discussion—using prompts at orientation, activation, and collaboration, teachers can track student progress toward developing efficacy.

Create a Best Fit Impact Model for Learning

Figure 5.7 illustrates four quadrants that represent a learner's progress and proficiency at a given time in a class. As discussed earlier in this chapter and in subsequent sections of this book, there are a few universals for learning, including developing strong teacher-student relations, providing clarity of learning intentions and success criteria, and developing student efficacy. Research also shows that students appear to move their learning forward at a greater rate when learning, instructional, and feedback strategies are aligned with levels of complexity (see Figure 1.1). In other words, there appear to be "anchor strategies" that are essential for all learners regardless of their progress and proficiency, and there are "best fit" strategies that have the highest probability (not a guarantee) of enhancing student learning relative to their current proficiency level.

Arguably, the best way to impact student learning is to start with understanding what strategies have substantially impacted student learning in the school context over time. Often those contextually based strategies have not been identified or clarified universally in a school or department. One way to begin the process of identifying and clarifying evidence-informed teaching strategies is to craft a team based BFIM. To start this process, a team may want to begin with research. However, the initial model should not be considered fixed, nor should the model be considered a requirement for teachers to use when teaching. The model should be adjusted based on data and a reference for making the best decisions for learners.

Figure 5.7 shows a template and Figure 5.8 illustrates an example of a BFIM (that may be utilized by a team; see Figure 1.15 for another example of a BFIM) for determining the best next step to improve student learning. Each team's or school's BFIM is expected to change over time as teachers collect data and review the strategies they are applying within their actual context.

Creating a Process for Collective Learning Through Teaming

Collective teacher efficacy is the most impactful influence on student achievement ever studied in education (Hattie, 2018). Collective efficacy may be best defined by Bandura (1993, 1997), who described the construct as "a group's shared belief in the conjoint capabilities to organize and execute the courses of action required to produce a given level of attainment." As such, collective teacher efficacy is the

Figure 5.7   Best Fit Impact Model Template

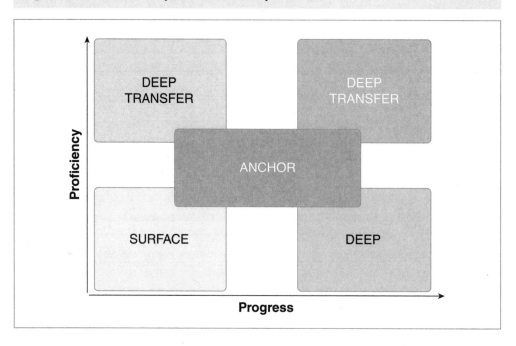

Figure 5.8   Best Fit Impact Model Example

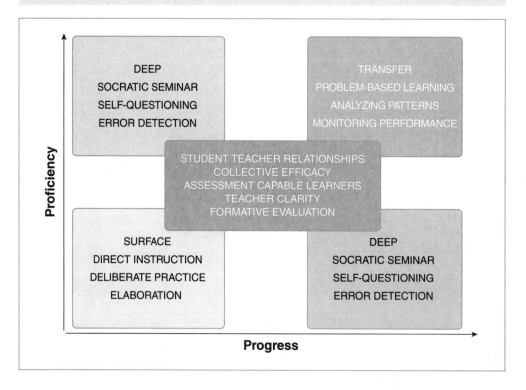

juxtaposition of the right beliefs and the right actions to substantially move student learning forward.

The previous section articulated the courses of action (utilizing progress and proficiency data to improve teaching and learning) required and the given level of attainment (i.e., more than one year's growth in one year's time in developing expertise and efficacy). This section focuses on the utilization of teams to cultivate the right beliefs and actions to meet the goal of substantial improvement in learning.

Defining Teams

The primary function of a team in schools is to substantially *cause* learning for learners and educators. Teams may be best defined as a small number of people who have a common purpose to work together, hold one another accountable to goals, and possess and develop an expertise to accomplish goals (Katzenbach & Smith, 1995). The demands of teachers to ensure substantial progress and proficiency of students across levels of complexity in learning (surface, deep, and transfer) and efficacy (orientation, activation, and collaboration) may be best met by having teachers form a team to support and challenge one another to meet such demands.

Teams have the promise to be incredibly effective for boosting morale by minimizing anonymity, increasing learning by promoting feedback and challenging bias, and enhancing effectiveness and efficiency in tackling ill structured problems. Such knowledge on the collective power of teachers to produce substantial learning for children has been well documented and advocated for (DuFour, DuFour, Eaker, Many, & Mattos, 2016). In today's economy, a plethora of organizations are approaching work from the vantage point of work groups and teams to tackle the complexities of contemporary work (Lawler, as cited in Dumaine, 1994; Senge, 1994). Countless studies have argued that work groups and teams are a critical element of the modern business environment (Hackman, 1987; Levi & Slem, 1995).

Team Process

In terms of establishing a process for inspecting and taking action on learner performance data, teams are advised to engage in a learning-centered team model, shown in Figure 5.9 and 5.10 respectively.

In order to develop effective teams that develop expertise and efficacy, teams need a process for determining, discussing and debating student and teacher efficacy and expertise, as well as designing

Figure 5.9   Learning-Centered Teaming Process

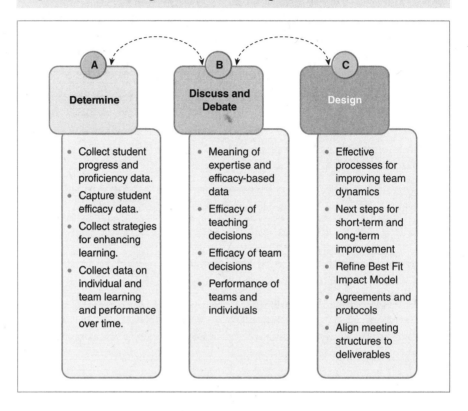

Figure 5.10   Learning-Centered Teaming Description

Three Steps	Expectations	Description
A **Determine**	• Collect student progress and proficiency data • Capture student efficacy data • Collect strategies for enhancing learning • Collect data on individual and team learning and performance over time	• This step is all about data collection related to student learning (efficacy and expertise), strategies that teachers have been using and the impact of those strategies, and the dynamics of the team and individual learning over the course of a school year. • This step answers the question: *Where are we now?*
	• Meaning of expertise and efficacy-based data	• This step is all about the individual teacher and teacher

Three Steps	Expectations	Description
B **Discuss and Debate**	• Effectiveness of unit and lesson design • Performance of teams and individuals	team interpretation of data. This is where debate, dialogue, and discussion are at the forefront of the teams work. Often the use of agreements, protocols, and differentiated meeting structures are beneficial for discussion and debate. (See Resource 6.13.c for an example of structured questions to prompt team discussion.) • This step answers the question: *Where are we now?*
C **Design**	• A lean/simple strategic plan • Best Fit Impact Model • Units and lessons that ensure transfer level learning • Effective processes for improving team dynamics	• This step is all about converting data through discussion and debate into a tangible product or deliverable to be used in later learning. • This step answer answers the questions: *Where are we going?* and, *What's next?*

solutions for improvement. Figure 5.10 illustrates a simple means for measuring individual and collective efficacy. Teams are advised to inspect their efficacy and determining next steps every 10 to 12 weeks. A series of strategies for enhancing team efficacy through collaboration is discussed in the next subsection.

Structuring the Methods for Determining, Discussing, Debating, and Designing Next Steps for Improvement

As stated, individual teacher and team activities and engagements should primary be utilized to *cause* learning. In other words, collaboration with others should be used to discuss student progress and proficiency to determine the impact teacher(s) have on students and what next steps need to be taken to improve learning. Topics such as logistical needs (ordering supplies, fixing the copier), textbook approvals, and debating classroom placements for the next school year should be removed from conversations that are intended to help children. The recommendation here is to center professional dialogue to questions associated with ensuring student efficacy and expertise.

Interestingly, teams are incredibly difficult to manage, and it is difficult to ensure high levels of performance with teams. As Lawler states, "Teams are the Ferraris of work design. They are high performance but high maintenance and expensive" (Lawler, as cited in Dumaine, 1994). Often team members do not, on their own, interact with one another to find the best solution but in fact work together to efficiently complete tasks. For example, in one study, teams did not negotiate diverse individual opinions and points of view to arrive at a collective opinion that prevails on its own merits; they found one idea and went with it to complete the task (Ochoa & Robinson, 2005). There are countless examples of this type of collective behavior that found that individuals in teams are often expected to conform to the group, and the group does not necessarily seek alternative solutions (Ochoa, Kelly, Stuart, & Rogers Adkinson, in press). The peculiarity in this result is that the individual who swayed the majority was not necessarily a particularly strong personality. In these studies, it appears that the majority was swayed by any demonstration of dissent. In summary, teams don't necessarily, on their own, learn. They learn by intentional design.

> Teams don't necessarily learn on their own. They learn by intentional design.

The idea that teams don't learn (or learn much) on their own without intentional design is important for those engaging in team development. In order for team-based work to be focused on student learning, teachers should consider organizing meetings based on the learning-centered team process steps the team is working on (determine, discussion and debate, and design) and ensure that scaffolds (agreements and protocols) are used to structure the discussions and decisions.

One of the most obvious points of a team is that they meet to collectively understand information and design next steps. The inflection point between data and design is discussing and debating information. This is one of the most difficult parts of teamwork (McDowell, 2009). In order for teams to discuss and debate effectively, teams should consider establishing agreements (or rules for engaging with others) and protocols (means for engaging in a conversation) into meetings. Furthermore, meetings should be centered on the needs of the team and nothing else! Figure 5.11 outlines a set of

Figure 5.11 Team Meeting Strategies Overview

	Meeting Structure	Agreements/Protocols	Deliverables
	The focus, time limit, and agenda must be clearly articulated for the team.	*The type of conversation warrants specific agreements and protocols.*	*The specific results of each meeting warrant different deliverables.*

C Design	• Once a year/semester
	• 2–3 hrs. long
		• The conversation is focused on long-term planning articulating specific areas of focus and means of measurement
		
		• Agreements
		  1. Share views and ask genuine questions
		  2. Explain reasoning and intent
		  3. Test assumptions and inferences
		  4. Use specific examples
		  5. Share all relevant information
		
		• Protocols
		  6. Resource 6.3 SWOT
		  7. Resource 6.4 Gap Analysis
		  8. Resource 6.6 Learning Dilemma
			• A plan of action

A Determine	• Quarterly
	• 1 hour long
		• The conversation is focused on current student progress and proficiency data and determining reasons for performance.
		
		• Agreements
		  1. Share views and ask genuine questions
		  2. Explain reasoning and intent
			• Student performance data
			• Group's facts, inference and potential next steps

(Continued)

Figure 5.11 (Continued)

	Meeting Structure	Agreements/Protocols	Deliverables
		3. Test assumptions and inferences 4. Use specific examples 5. Share all relevant information • Protocols (6.2, 6.3, 6.4) 6. What?, So What?, Now What? 7. SWOT 8. Gap analysis	
B **Discuss and Debate**	• Monthly • 30–45 minutes	• The conversation is focused on identifying strategies to implement and receiving professional support on developing, implementing, and refining practice. • Agreements 1. Share views and ask genuine questions 2. Explain reasoning and intent 3. Test assumptions and inferences 4. Use specific examples 5. Share all relevant information • Protocols 6.1, 6.2 6. Critical Friends 7. What?, So What?, Now What?	• Refined BFIM (key learning from the group is documented for future reference).

Each protocol can be to used to assist teachers in guiding conversations. They can all be found in the Appendix at the back of the book.

meeting structures, agreements and protocols, and deliverables that align to a set of questions. Each meeting structure is designed to meet the specific success criteria of the group.

Conclusion

The development of individual and collective efficacy of teachers is essential to the learning of students. As discussed in this chapter, collective efficacy has the highest likelihood of making a substantial impact on student learning. When teachers work together in teams to focus on ensuring students gain more than one year's growth in efficacy and expertise, there is high probability that learners and teachers will develop in their expertise and efficacy. This is easier said than done, as teams require established parameters for their work, an agreed upon process to engage in their work, and a means for developing their capacity to collaborate and problem solve.

---------- **REFLECTION QUESTIONS** ----------

- What are the "core tasks" that your team focuses on when meeting over the school year? How do these "core tasks" relate to the suggested focus on progress and proficiency of student efficacy and expertise?

- Does your team typically measure their team's individual and collective efficacy? (see Figure 5.1 and Figure 5.2)

- Where do you think your team is (or, if you have evidence, where is your team) along the individual and collective efficacy progression (introduction, application, or reinforcing)?

- Does your team have a BFIM? If not, what steps would you take to begin to develop a BFIM?

- How does your team's process for learning compare and contrast with the suggested process in this chapter?

- How does your team currently structure collaboration when debating and making decisions? Does your team using agreement, protocols, meetings, and creating deliverables?

- How does your team currently structure meetings? How does that structure relate to the meeting structure proposed in this book? How would changes in your meetings be a benefit to your team?

ACTIVITIES

ACTIVITY 5.1

Review the agenda notes for the past six department and staff meetings. How would those meetings have run differently if they had been structured using Team Meeting Strategies in Figure 5.11? Next, determine what steps your team needs to take to improve individual and team learning.

ACTIVITY 5.2

Ask your team to identify possible ways to determine and take action on progress, proficiency, and complexity of learning for the team and in each classroom. Questions to consider include the following:

1. **Progress:** *How do we know if students are getting more than one year's growth in one year's time in our classrooms? What outcomes are critical for us to track growth? How do we discuss this growth with each other and our learners? How do they track their own learning? Once we know that information, what will we do individually, collectively, and with students?*

2. **Proficiency:** *How do we know if students are proficient in their learning? Do we all have a similar criteria for proficiency? How does this level of proficiency relate to complexity of learning (surface, deep, and transfer)? How do we maintain progress as a priority over proficiency? What implications does this have on our classroom rules and our reporting (grading)? How do we involve students?*

3. **Complexity:** *How do we discuss levels of learning (surface, deep, and transfer) as a team? How does this relate to our understanding of student progress and proficiency? How do we ensure that each level of learning (i.e., surface, deep, and transfer) is a key part of our teaching practice and our discussions as a team? How are our students involved in the discussion of leveled-success criteria (surface, deep, and transfer)?*

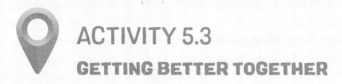

ACTIVITY 5.3

GETTING BETTER TOGETHER

One way to begin developing collective efficacy is to engage in the Learning Rounds process and then use the resources in Chapters 2 and Chapter 3 to improve student efficacy. Figure 5.12 illustrates a sample visual cue that one teacher created and then shared with other faculty members. To ensure students are making progress toward developing orientation, you may want to collect data via learning rounds before and after implementing new strategies.

Figure 5.12   **Visual Display of Surface, Deep, and Transfer**

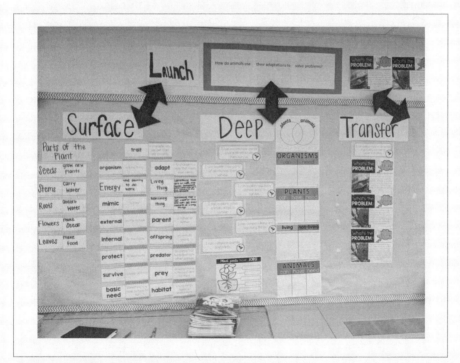

Source: Ross School; Ross, CA. Used with Permission.

NEXT STEPS

- Review your team's "core tasks" and identify steps that your team needs to take to focus work on progress and proficiency of student learning.

- Create a BFIM with other team members.

- Review the agreements and protocols offered in this book and compare those agreements and protocols with your team's processes for discussion and problem-solving. Determine if your team's approach to collaboration needs to change.

- Share your learning of this chapter with colleagues and students.

CONCLUSION

At the beginning of this book, I included a quote from Malcolm Gladwell about T. E. Lawrence—or colloquially, Lawrence of Arabia. The quote was to illustrate that the strategies that make the greatest impact in learning and in life are often those that are hardest to implement, requiring tremendous endurance on the part of the teacher and student, and are often counterintuitive in the field of education. Such strategies are often deemed underdog strategies. As a school administrator, I have strategically planned and implemented on a daily basis these underdog strategies in high-poverty and high-privilege schools, each with a beginning narrative that these strategies would not work and it would be better to double down on those strategies that have been "known" in our industry to have worked (i.e., the frontrunner strategies). In each of these systems, the students under my care showed substantial growth in their learning and in their efficacy to learn and continue to learn. Moreover, so has my staff. Lawrence of Arabia used strategies to conquer the port of Aqaba by crossing the desert in the middle of summer. He fought against traditional tactics, comfort, and symbols of strength and challenged the assumptions of his enemy—*no one would cross the desert*. I have decided as a leader and teacher to cross the desert in the field of education. To buck the trend of focusing on school structures, such as bell schedules and classroom design and curriculum planning and focus on developing efficacy and expertise.

This book is about crossing the desert and using strategies that have a substantial impact on learning and admitting that these approaches are indeed incredibly difficult to execute and are, for the most part, uncommon in schools. We often do not discuss and implement strategies associated with efficacy of students, nor design the ways in which we debate as adults, nor ensure students develop surface-, deep-, and transfer-level learning. In the introduction, I discussed that the development of efficacy must be a collective effort between students and teachers. I argued that we shouldn't treat students as experts but rather develop their expertise. This requires us to not hand control of learning over to students but to work with them as a shared responsibility, a shared journey.

We looked at a framework for developing expert learners, creating a culture of efficacy and expertise, approaching curriculum design using rapid prototyping units and lessons for impact, and exploring instructional approaches for impacting student learning through teaching. These elements are fundamentally based on the most substantial research to date and are underpinned by what we know in cognitive psychology. They are our best bet to improving learning. We also discussed the importance of building teacher individual and collective efficacy to enhance learning so teachers and students share in the journey of improvement together.

Educators need to enable students to strike a balance between underdog and frontrunner strategies to impact their own learning—to develop expertise and walk in the shoes of experts, to live their lives to experience their surroundings, and to tackle some of their problems over time. This moves students to developing the capacity of knowing what to do when they don't know what to do. Over time, they have the knowledge and skills and efficacy through experience and education to navigate uncertainty and create new solutions from the iterations of the past and the present conditions they face—that's an expert and that's what we should be developing in students as educators.

I look to others and their expertise to support all of us, including me, in building efficacious, expertise-laden systems for all children.

AFTERWORD

When we think about helping our children develop expertise, we learn that we are faced with a mass of research, tips, and strategies: an overwhelming base of findings. As we know, almost everything works. This book has taken us through a journey of organization of the best and most significantly evidenced studies and the most pertinent and relevant strategies and linked them with more examples of how to implement strategies into practice than we could ever dream of finding in one book.

We gain insight when McDowell tells us that deliberate practice also needs deliberate experimentation for deeper learning to occur. We should not be so tied to our syllabus that we constrain the processes necessary of trial and error and thinking outside the box, which empower and assist deep understanding.

Our quest is to take students from surface, to deep, through to transfer—each equally weighted, each combining to make learners proficient and self-regulated. This is carried through into copious staff development meeting strategies and well thought-out, detailed discussion grids focusing on our own parallel reflection and self-regulation. We are given different pathways—one pathway leads us down the path of beginning with application or transfer: We see what happens then move to surface learning, to deep, then to transfer. This is a common strategy in far Eastern countries in mathematics and echoes Paul Innis's work with science contexts in which we start with the end result, then work with students, along with our own observations, to inform what surface learning is needed before we venture into deep and transfer. Another pathway starts with surface then moves to deep and transfer—we see that the subject, the context, and student needs determine which pathway to take.

The well-researched conceptual framework of formative assessment (what happens in the moment to ensure effective student learning) gives shape and coherence to the chapters, focusing on culture, prior knowledge, goals, and ongoing student and teacher feedback.

The rigorous research findings of the visible learning principles, originated from John Hattie's work, combine with formative assessment to strengthen the path outlined.

Ausubel's instruction that we should ascertain what the child knows then teach accordingly is our starting point in the classroom. McDowell says our plans should be "etched in sand," not stone, so that we can respond to students' prior knowledge and teach accordingly, not just at the beginnings of lessons, but throughout the learning process, using tried and tested strategies to elicit student understanding as often as we can.

The book emphasizes that it is essential students know the learning intentions and success criteria, and throughout, we have seen contextualized lesson ideas illustrated by possible surface, deep and transfer success criteria. The point here is that sometimes this will aid differentiation, but if we want to have the highest expectations, this book can show us how to progress a series of lessons so that all students reach transfer. The evidence about the limitations of our working memories is referenced in situations where we need to make sure students are not overwhelmed with information or tasks: We see that strategies such as success criteria help in the task of keeping Bjork's "desirable difficulties" (Bjork, 1994, pp. 185–205) in place while organizing student thinking so that working memory is freed up.

Nottingham's learning pit illustrates the challenge and struggle in learning, the importance of making mistakes, and the strategies for climbing out. Posters from real classrooms bring this to life.

Nuthall's work, as we are reminded, tells us that students often give each other misinformation, but hope is at hand when we see that the outcome is more positive if peer explanation takes place during the deep and transfer stages of learning rather than during the surface, where limited experience causes some disconnects.

We end with a summary of the main points in McDowell's message that we can think of three levels: orientation, activation, and collaboration. The first level is student awareness of learning intentions and how they are learning at any one point. The second is the importance of metacognition and students knowing how to learn and what strategies might help them. Collaboration reflects Hattie's number one (at this moment) effect size of all the influences on learning: effective collective self-efficacy. When teachers work together believing and proving that they are making a difference to student learning, student expertise will follow, both at the student and teacher level. We see McDowell's four elements—push, pull, press, and pause—when to encourage, when to hold back, and so on. The last section and the full appendix gives us a comprehensive pack of activities, templates, and reflection questions to ensure teacher development also follows surface, deep, and transfer paths. The message is clear—what we want from students, we need also as a staff of teachers, a mirrored image of shared culture and practice.

McDowell gives us examples of whole units of work, of possible lessons, and of means to run staff meetings to impact student learning in such careful detail that we have the tools to begin developing student expertise, knowing the theory but linked with powerful examples. This book could have been an interesting academic discourse, but it is, instead, a vehicle for whole school development, designed to be useful at all levels. As I said to the author, "This is a tour de force to be reckoned with . . . "

—Shirley Clarke
International freelance consultant and bestselling author
www.shirleyclarke-education.org

RESOURCES

Conditions for Impact Resources

- Resource 6.1: Critical Friends Protocol
- Resource 6.2: What? So What? Now What? Protocol
- Resource 6.3: SWOT Analysis Protocol
- Resource 6.4: Gap Analysis Protocol
- Resource 6.5: Constructivist Tuning Protocol
- Resource 6.6: Learning Dilemma Protocol
- Resource 6.7: Constructivist Listening Protocol

Planning for Impact Resources

- Resource 6.8: Leveled Success Criteria Development Process
- Resource 6.9: Transfer Task Resources

Teaching for Impact Resources

- Resource 6.10: The Fundamentals Routine
- Resource 6.11: Video Reflection Protocol

Collective Efficacy: Developing Efficacy and Expertise as Professionals

- Resource 6.12: Tools for Measuring Efficacy and Expertise
  - Resource 6.12a: Effect Size Tool
  - Resource 6.12b: Knowledge Gain Tool
  - Resource 6.12c: Survey Tool Example
  - Resource 6.12d: Focus Group Activity
  - Resource 6.12e: Interview Activity

- Resource 6.13: Examples of Data Collection and Analysis Tools

Conditions for Impact Resources

Resource 6.1

Critical Friends Protocol

Purpose: The following protocol is designed to provide students and educators with specific feedback regarding a product, presentation, or process.

45 minutes

Opening Moves (Introduction) **(5 minutes)**

- Review the purpose of the protocol.

- Review agreements (or norms) of the team.

- Identify facilitator/participant and participant.

- Review success criteria of product, process, or presentation being evaluated.

Opening Presentation **(5 minutes)**

- The teacher or student requesting feedback provides a 10-minute over-view on the product, process, or presentation.

- The facilitator will then ask the CFT for any clarifying questions.

- The presenter will provide answers to any clarifying question.

- *This process can be much more effective when materials are provided before the CFT Review. One suggestion is to email all CFT members with materials to be reviewed 72 hours before the CFT process.*

Strengths (I like) **(10 minutes)**

- Facilitator asks the CFT to provide feedback related to the strengths of the product, process, or presentation.

- CFT members will begin each piece of feedback using the following stems: "I like . . . because_____," or "One strength is . . . because___." (Rationale should be related to success criteria.)

- *During the next two sections (Questions and Next Steps), the teacher receiving feedback should not make any remarks and should only listen and write down notes.*

- *The facilitator should ensure that all information is posted on the website.*

(Continued)

(Continued)

Questions (I wonder)

- Facilitator asks the CFT to provide questions for the teacher-presenter to think through the product, process, or presentation.

- CFT members will begin each piece of feedback using the following stems: "I wonder because___," or "One question to consider includes___." (Rationale should be related to success criteria.)

Next Steps

- Facilitator asks the presenter to articulate next steps in light of the information he/she received from the CFT.

Closing Remarks

- The teacher states "thank you" for the feedback.

Closing Moves **(5 minutes)**

- Ask participants to rate how well the team executed the protocol and followed agreements.

Copyright © 2019 by Corwin. All rights reserved. Reprinted from *Developing Expert Learners: A Roadmap for Growing Confident and Competent Students* by Michael McDowell. Thousand Oaks, CA: Corwin, www.corwin.com. Reproduction authorized for educational use by educators, local school sites, and/or noncommercial or nonprofit entities that have purchased the book.

Resource 6.2

What? So What? Now What? Protocol

The following protocol allows participants to separate observations and facts from inferences/assumptions in order to make effective individual and collective decisions.

45 minutes

Opening Moves (Introduction) **(5 minutes)**

- Review the purpose of the protocol.
- Review agreements (or norms) of the team.
- Identify facilitator/participant and participant.

Statements of Problem/Challenge/ Circumstance **(10 minutes)**

- The facilitator asks a participant to outline a current challenge/problem/ or circumstance.
- The facilitator asks for clarifying questions from other participants.
- The facilitator then asks everyone to identify the facts of the challenge/ problem/circumstance (What do we know are facts from this challenge?).
- The facilitator populates that information onto a chart under the term "What."

Mastering Our Stories—*So What?* **(10 minutes)**

- The facilitator then asks what appears to be inferences/assumptions that are drawn from the challenge (What are we assuming or taking for granted? What other assumptions may there be?). The facilitator populates this information onto a chart under the term "So What."
- The facilitator asks the participants to consider all of the people who are impacted by this challenge and identify what assumptions they may possess in this challenge.

Taking Action—*Now What?* **(10 minutes)**

- Next, the facilitator asks each participant to write down three or four specific next steps on Post-it Notes. The facilitator provides the following prompts (What additional information do we need? What assumptions

(Continued)

(Continued)

do we need to check? What appear to be logical next steps in moving toward a solution?).

- The facilitator asks the participants to silently place their Post-it Notes under a column entitled "Next Steps." Participants may group the Post-it Notes quietly.

- The facilitator then asks the group to describe the groupings. (What appear to be the major themes related to next steps?)

- The facilitator asks the original participant if they would like to share next steps they are considering.

- The facilitator then asks the original participant when they should check back on action steps and outcomes.

- The session is then closed.

Closing Moves **(5 minutes)**

- Ask participants to rate how well the team executed the protocol and followed agreements.

Copyright © 2019 by Corwin. All rights reserved. Reprinted from *Developing Expert Learners: A Roadmap for Growing Confident and Competent Students* by Michael McDowell. Thousand Oaks, CA: Corwin, www.corwin.com. Reproduction authorized for educational use by educators, local school sites, and/or noncommercial or nonprofit entities that have purchased the book.

Resource 6.3

SWOT Analysis Protocol

The following protocol allows participants to evaluate strengths, weaknesses, opportunities, and threats that are critical for analyzing internal and external constraints.

45 minutes

Opening Moves (Introduction) **(5 minutes)**

- Review the purpose of the protocol.

- Review agreements (or norms) of the team.

- Identify facilitator/participant and participant.

- Post chart and label with the following words: "Strengths," "Weaknesses," "Opportunities," and "Threats." See the figure below for an exemplar.

SWOT Analysis Template

Strengths	Weaknesses
Opportunities	Threats

Statements of Problem/Challenge/Circumstance **(10 minutes)**

- Present the idea/challenge or circumstance.

- Discuss the need to identify potential strengths/weaknesses/opportunities/threats.

- Participants should form into small groups of three to four.

Group Development **(10 minutes)**

- Groups begin developing ideas (typically on Post-its) and including them under each of the four quadrants of the matrix.

(Continued)

(Continued)

Collective Group Discussion **(10 minutes)**

- Everyone comes back and discusses the following questions:

  1. What key ideas stand out? What surprises you?

  2. What inferences emerge? What themes and patterns emerge? What implications to our organization can we draw?

  3. What can we do with this information? What next steps do you recommend?

Copyright © 2019 by Corwin. All rights reserved. Reprinted from *Developing Expert Learners: A Roadmap for Growing Confident and Competent Students* by Michael McDowell. Thousand Oaks, CA: Corwin, www.corwin.com. Reproduction authorized for educational use by educators, local school sites, and/or noncommercial or nonprofit entities that have purchased the book.

Resource 6.4

Gap Analysis Protocol

The following protocol allows participants to identify the differences between the desired outcome and current performance or actual state of affairs.

35 minutes

Opening Moves (Introduction) **(5 minutes)**

- Review the purpose of the protocol.
- Review agreements (or norms) of the team.
- Identify facilitator/participant and participant.

Statements of Problem/Challenge/Circumstance **(15 minutes)**

- Ask participants to identify the ideal state or outcome (desired) they are trying to reach. Provide a scenario, review reference documents, or offer a general description.
- Ask participants to define the actual or current state/performance level at this point in time.

Next Steps **(15 minutes)**

- Ask participants what can be done to alleviate the discrepancy between the ideal state and current state/performance level.
- Identify five key steps the organization could take now.

Gap Analysis Template

Current	Next Steps	Desired

(Continued)

(Continued)

Gap Analysis Example

Current	**Next Steps**	**Desired**
Learning intentions and success criteria are unfamiliar terminology to students and staff.	Showcase internal successes (7th grade teams).	Ensure clear learning intentions and success criteria are differentiated between surface, deep, and transfer levels of learning.
Assessment tools do not articulate surface-, deep-, and transfer-learning expectations.	Provide explicit P.D. on instructional strategies at surface level.	High impact strategies at surface level are utilized.
Instruction is primarily focused on deeper learning methodologies.		

Copyright © 2019 by Corwin. All rights reserved. Reprinted from *Developing Expert Learners: A Roadmap for Growing Confident and Competent Students* by Michael McDowell. Thousand Oaks, CA: Corwin, www.corwin.com. Reproduction authorized for educational use by educators, local school sites, and/or noncommercial or nonprofit entities that have purchased the book.

Resource 6.5

Constructivist Tuning Protocol

Purpose: The following protocol provides a process for people to give and receive feedback to one another.

Suggested Time: 45 minutes

Opening Moves (Introduction) **(5 minutes)**

- Review the purpose of the protocol.
- Review agreements (or norms) of the team.
- Identify facilitator/participant and participant.
- Review success criteria of product, process, or presentation being evaluated.

Procedure

Step 1: Introduction: The facilitator states to the group that the presenter has 10 minutes to present their work to others. This is an opportunity for the participants to provide context for their work and their areas of interest for feedback. No interruptions or questions are allowed, just listening and note-taking by the participants (10 minutes). After 10 minutes, the facilitator asks the participants if they have any clarifying questions. The facilitator typically provides 3 to 4 minutes for clarifying questions.

Step 2: Feedback: The facilitator thanks the presenter for presenting and then tells the presenter that they will now listen and record feedback and will not respond to any comments. For 2 minutes, participants review their notes and collect their thoughts on feedback they can give that would be most helpful to the presenter.Next, the facilitator asks for "Warm Feedback": Participants share the evidence they found were strengths in the presentation (5 minutes). Next the facilitator asks for "Cool Feedback": Participants share questions that arise and feedback to move their work toward success criteria (5 minutes).

Step 3: Next Steps: Presenter takes a few minutes to review the feedback and to consider his or her response (2–3 minutes).

Presenter responds to those comments and questions that he or she chooses. Participants are silent (5 minutes).

(Continued)

(Continued)

Closing Moves **(5 minutes)**

- Ask participants to rate how well the team executed the protocol and followed agreements.

Copyright © 2019 by Corwin. All rights reserved. Reprinted from *Developing Expert Learners: A Roadmap for Growing Confident and Competent Students* by Michael McDowell. Thousand Oaks, CA: Corwin, www.corwin.com. Reproduction authorized for educational use by educators, local school sites, and/or noncommercial or nonprofit entities that have purchased the book.

Resource 6.6

Learning Dilemma Protocol

Purpose: The following protocol provides individuals with a structured process for students, teachers, and leaders to think through a challenge in a collaborative setting.

45 minutes

Opening Moves (Introduction) **(5 minutes)**

- Review the purpose of the protocol.

- Review agreements (or norms) of the team.

- Identify facilitator/presenter and reviewers.

Statements of Dilemma **(10 minutes)**

- The facilitator asks the presenter to present a dilemma to others. The presenter briefly explains the dilemma and addresses the following questions: *Why is this important? Why is this a dilemma? How is this a dilemma? What is causing this dilemma? (Presenter may bring exemplars/artifacts.)*

- The facilitator asks the group to provide any clarifying questions to the presenter.

Discussing Dilemma **(10 minutes)**

- Facilitator asks the presenter to write notes and not speak during the next 10 minutes.

- The group discusses the dilemma. The group discussion typically addresses the following questions: *What are the important facts that have emerged in this dilemma? What are the assumptions underlying the dilemma? What are potential perspectives or questions that may be of value to consider?*

Reflection From Presenter **(10 minutes)**

- Presenter has an opportunity to share reflections and next steps.

(Continued)

(Continued)

Reflection on Process

- The facilitator asks the presenter and the group the following questions: What were the strengths in our adherence to the protocol? How could we improve our process?

Closing Moves **(5 minutes)**

- Ask participants to rate how well the team executed the protocol and followed agreements.

Copyright © 2019 by Corwin. All rights reserved. Reprinted from *Developing Expert Learners: A Roadmap for Growing Confident and Competent Students* by Michael McDowell. Thousand Oaks, CA: Corwin, www.corwin.com. Reproduction authorized for educational use by educators, local school sites, and/or noncommercial or nonprofit entities that have purchased the book.

Resource 6.7

Constructivist Listening Protocol

Constructivist Listening

The following protocol supports group members in preparing for listening in a group setting.

10 minutes

Opening Moves (Introduction) **(5 minutes)**

- Review the purpose of protocol.
- Review agreements (or norms) of the team.
- Identify facilitator/participant and participant.

Review Norms and Guidelines

Norm: I agree to listen and think about you in exchange for you doing the same for me.

Guidelines: Each person . . .

- Has equal time to talk
- Does not interrupt, give advice, or break in with a personal story
- Agrees that confidentiality is maintained
- Does not criticize or complain about others during their time to talk

Preparation

- Facilitator asks each participant to find a partner.
- Next, the facilitator presents a prompt for each participant to share with the other (*e.g., What is on top for you? What do you need to discuss to be fully present for today's work? What are you looking forward to today? What are you confused by or challenged by?*)

First Cycle

- The facilitator asks the first participant to share their response with the second participant.

(Continued)

(Continued)

Second Cycle

- The facilitator states, "switch," and asks the second participant to share their response with the first participant.

Closing Moves **(5 minutes)**

- Ask participants to rate how well the team executed the protocol and followed agreements.

Derived from National School Reform Faculty, Harmony Education Center (2018)

Copyright © 2019 by Corwin. All rights reserved. Reprinted from *Developing Expert Learners: A Roadmap for Growing Confident and Competent Students* by Michael McDowell. Thousand Oaks, CA: Corwin, www.corwin.com. Reproduction authorized for educational use by educators, local school sites, and/or noncommercial or nonprofit entities that have purchased the book.

Planning for Impact Resources

Leveled Success Criteria Development Process

Option A

The process for designing leveled success criteria is a simple six-step process:

Step 1: Craft learning intentions in student friendly language

Take the outcomes of your syllabus and convert them into "I will" statements for learners. Ensure that the verb that is used after "I will" requires deep or transfer expectations
Example: *I will* apply multiplication of fractions.

Step 2: Craft leveled success criteria at surface, deep, and transfer learning

Once you establish your learning intention, you will need to create success criteria to ensure students know what they need to know to be able to meet your expectations. When writing out your expectations, you want to use verbs at each level of learning (i.e., surface, deep, and transfer) (see Figure 3.6 *Leveled Success Criteria Rhetoric Tool* for exemplar verbs at surface, deep, and transfer level expectations).

Step 3: Refine learning intentions by ensuring the verbs are aligned to deep or transfer and refine success criteria by removing tasks, activities, and contexts.

Once you have sketched your learning intentions and leveled success criteria, it's a good idea to review your work and ensure you have alignment of verbs and expectations at each level of the success criteria and that your learning intentions is written at the highest level of learning you expect.
In addition, you will want to ensure that your success criteria don't include assignments or products in the descriptors. Assignments, products,

(Continued)

(Continued)

and activities are all ways in which students demonstrate their learning, but more often than not, they are not learning intentions nor success criteria. For example, if students are learning to write a balanced argument, then we want to include the criteria that is necessary in such an argument, including forming an opinion in the closing, relating two opinions, and backing up opinions by experts. We would not want to include in the success criteria "write a paper." The paper is a task in which students will demonstrate the success criteria. The success criteria are what we want students to focus on during class and when writing a paper.

Step 4: Create a driving question that presents students a rationale for meeting transfer expectations.

This may be viewed as an optional step, but it is actual critical in presenting the learning intention as important for learning. Driving questions position the learning intention as a question rather than a statement and often show students one or more contexts (or situations) in which they, the students, will engage to meet the learning intention. Driving questions are usually presented to students at the beginning of a unit to drive the learning.

How do we apply multiplication of fractions [when converting units in chemistry to demonstrate the relationships between quantities]?

Step 5: Receive feedback from peers to ensure alignment of learning intentions and success criteria.

Before building other parts of your unit (such as building tasks and activities for kids), ask colleagues to review your work and look for the following:

- Learning intentions: Does the learning intention require deep and transfer learning?

- Success criteria: Do the success criteria align to surface, deep, and transfer? Are the success criteria devoid of contexts and tasks?

- Driving question: Does the driving question align to the learning intention? Does it require a student to learn at surface, deep, and transfer to answer?

Option B

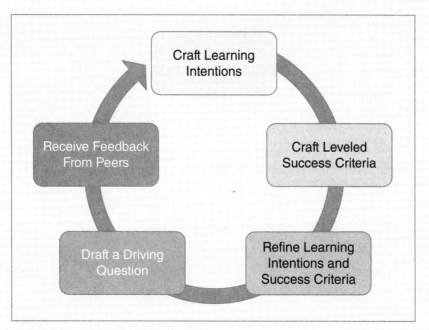

Leveled success criteria ensure that students are aware of complexity and that all students are meeting complex expectations. This simple strategy may assist your learners in developing their ability to become their own teachers.

Copyright © 2019 by Corwin. All rights reserved. Reprinted from *Developing Expert Learners: A Roadmap for Growing Confident and Competent Students* by Michael McDowell. Thousand Oaks, CA: Corwin, www.corwin.com. Reproduction authorized for educational use by educators, local school sites, and/or noncommercial or nonprofit entities that have purchased the book.

Resource 6.9

Transfer Task Resources

One area that must be emphasized and discussed amongst teams is how to prepare students to meet transfer-level expectations.

In 2018, the Organisation for Economic Co-operation and Development (2018) submitted a new global competence framework entitled *Preparing Our Youth for an Inclusive and Sustainable World.* The Programme for International Student Assessment (PISA) has stated that they will begin assessing student competency in a series of areas including the following:

- Examine[ing] local, global, and intercultural issues

- Understand[ing] and appreciat[ing] the perspectives and worldviews of others

- Tak[ing] action for collective well-being and sustainable development

- Engag[ing] in open, appropriate and effective interactions across cultures (pp. 7–8)

These competencies may be viewed as articulating what types of tasks students should solve (i.e., Examine local, global, and intercultural issues and take action for collective well-being and sustainable development.) and how students should approach such tasks (i.e., Understand and appreciate the perspectives and worldviews of others and engage in open, appropriate, and effective interactions across cultures.). As Fullan and Quinn (2018) have reported, learning today requires interactions between students, including teams, to solve ambiguous and complex real-world problems that impact human and environmental sustainability and to approach such problems by understanding and appreciating various perspectives and preparing to engage in open, appropriate, and effective interactions across cultures. This book translates these aspirations into practical applications by embedding this work into the design of (1) the classroom culture, (2) unit and lesson planning, and (3) instruction to ensure student tackle transfer-level work by requiring students to tackle questions and situations that are purposeful and provocative, perplexing problems, and perspective laden.

The challenge for teachers is twofold:

1. Teachers have often not received training, feedback, and coaching on designing and implementing transfer-level experiences and expectations for learners.

2. Teachers need concrete, practical steps for implementing these types of experiences and tasks for students and to ensure students, in fact, rise to the occasion.

Teachers must carve out time in professional learning experiences with colleagues to review student performance data, units and lessons, tasks, and instructional practices that are aimed to meet transfer-level demands and determine the quality of those experiences for learners and their ability to transfer over time. This text has offered several examples for preparing and ensuring students meet transfer-level expectations. Resources 6.9a, 6.9b, and 6.9c illustrate tools that teachers may use to support students in engaging in transfer work (Resource 6.9a) or to gauge the effectiveness of transfer-level work expectations for learners (Resources 6.9b and 6.9c).

Resource 6.9a   Purposeful and Perplexing Task Strategies

Routine	Description	Example
Got Glocal?	• Students review the local and global implications of a problem or problems.	• Students explore the themes and patterns of a problem or problems around the globe.
Charge it up	• Students explore the cost/benefits from stakeholders on a problem or problems.	• Students engage in a stakeholder analysis of a problem or problems.
Why is this an issue?	• Students find out the underlying reasons for an issue or issues.	• Students ask the 5 "Whys" to get to the heart of the key problem.

(Continued)

(Continued)

Resource 6.9b   Evaluation of Transfer Tasks

	Not Met	Met	Exceeded
Perplexing		• Tasks align to key learning intentions that are central to core discipline(s). • Tasks require students to apply success criteria at surface and deep learning. • Student identifies changes in the problem situation that would require new or additional tasks. • Student identifies relationship of learning intention, success criteria, and issue(s) in different contexts. • Student identifies changes in the problem situation that would impact the solution.	
Purposeful and Provocative		• Identifies contexts and issues that relate to established transfer-level success criteria. • Creates driving questions that relate to key issues and transfer-level success criteria. • Identifies tasks (i.e., reading, writing, and talking) that meet transfer-level success criteria.	
Perspective		• Identifies various values, perspectives, and beliefs that are connected to this context/issue.	

Resource 6.9c Transfer Checklist

Transfer-Level Expectations	Checklist
Purposeful and Provocative	Are the students facing a question that is relevant to them individually, to their peers or community, and/or to the broader world? Are students facing a problem or question that evokes passion and emotion?
Perplexing	Does the learner face a change to parts of a presented problem, a complete change to the situation/context, or in the task that they are developing?
Perspective Laden	Does the learner bring to bear multiple perspectives to understand and address a problem or question?

Copyright © 2019 by Corwin. All rights reserved. Reprinted from *Developing Expert Learners: A Roadmap for Growing Confident and Competent Students* by Michael McDowell. Thousand Oaks, CA: Corwin, www.corwin.com. Reproduction authorized for educational use by educators, local school sites, and/or noncommercial or nonprofit entities that have purchased the book.

Teaching for Impact Resources

Resource 6.10

The Fundamentals Routine

The following routine is executed as follows:

Beginning of a unit of learning

1. Teacher asks learners to review the learning intentions and success criteria.

2. Teachers then engage in a pre-assessment with learners on their current knowledge and skills relative to the learning intentions and success criteria. This step may include looking at exemplar work to determine current performance.

3. Students highlight their current performance and set goals for learning.

During the unit of learning

4. Teachers establish times throughout the unit for students to review their current performance related to success criteria and ask students to determine if they are on track to meet the success criteria. Students discuss their current progress with other students and give and receive feedback on their progress, proficiency, efficacy of meeting goals, and potential next steps to maintain or improve performance (typically this feedback process is structured by using a protocol, such as the Critical Friends process).

Conclusion of the unit of learning

5. Teachers ask students to take a post-assessment and then reflect on progress and proficiency in their learning. Students often review their work with peers and discuss strengths, challenges, and potential next steps.

Figure 6.10a   Learner Reflection on Learning Example I

<u>**Learning Reflections**</u>

Dear Parents, I am so exited for you to Be here tonigth I can show you all of the work I've done this year. I have worked very hard on it and had fun doing it. I hope You like it!

Tools I regularly use in my learning for:

<u>Where I am:</u> looking at my <u>pre</u> and <u>post</u> <u>test</u>, getting feedBack, and help from a partner!!

<u>Where I am going:</u> success criteria and goals

<u>How will I get there:</u> Practice steps, help from teacher, slow thinking!!

Experiences that have inspired me as a learner: my Passion Project inspired me because I enjoy doing it and I can learn aBout things I've never even heard of.

Experiences that have challenged me as a learner: when I learned discs in addition it was challenging, but when I practiced more, I got better and understand it!

I know I am in the learning zone because: am not panicking and I am Being challenged and it's, fun but not <u>easy</u>.

When I am in the learning pit, I use these tools to move forward:
• Bely Breath • <u>rered</u> the directions
• think slower • using strategies and taking a break.

(Continued)

(Continued)

Figure 6.10b   Learner Reflection on Learning Example II

<u>**Learning Reflections**</u>

Dear Parents,

I am so happy, I can't wait to see you and I think you will be proud of my <u>growth</u>!

Love you ♡

Tools I regularly use in my learning for:

<u>Where I am:</u> looking at my **pre** and **post** tests, examples, feedback, success criteria, thumbus

<u>Where I am going:</u> success criteria, goals,

<u>How will I get there:</u> practice steps, help from my learning partner

Experiences that have inspired me as a learner:
One time I asked my learning partner for my opening sentence and I was moving forward in my learning. My partner and I also got inspired.

Experiences that have challenged me as a learner:
I was challenged because I felt like I could never do a math problem with a certain strategy, but then I finally got the hang of it!!

I know I am in the learning zone because:
can tell when it's uncomfortable sometimes, but most of the time I <u>eventually</u> get the hang of it.

When I am in the learning pit, I use these tools to move forward:
- Think about somthing that you are good at then come back to the subject later.
-
- feedback!!
- privacy board
- break out desk
- reread
- use groth mindset

Copyright © 2019 by Corwin. All rights reserved. Reprinted from *Developing Expert Learners: A Roadmap for Growing Confident and Competent Students* by Michael McDowell. Thousand Oaks, CA: Corwin, www.corwin.com. Reproduction authorized for educational use by educators, local school sites, and/or non-commercial or nonprofit entities that have purchased the book.

Resource 6.11

Video Reflection Protocol

Purpose

45 minutes

Opening Moves (Introduction) (5 minutes)

- Review the purpose of the protocol.

- Review agreements (or norms) of the team.

- Identify facilitator/participant and participant.

Procedure

- The facilitator shows a video of a teacher teaching in the classroom.

- The participants answer the question that follow.

- The facilitator then asks the teacher in the film to present his/her core purpose for the video (e.g., What they were looking to do accomplish?).

- The facilitator asks for clarifying questions.

- The participants watch the video again, looking to deepen their responses based on specific "'look fors" from the teacher.

- The facilitator then follows the "What? So What? Now What?" protocol.

Teacher: _____

Grade/Subject Matter: **Date:**   **Time:**

How do students demonstrate that they are clear about what they are learning and what success looks like?

(Continued)

(Continued)

Do the students know where they are going? Where they are now? What steps do they need to take to move forward in their learning?

Who does the talking? What is the balance between teacher talk and student talk?

Which students are actively supporting one another in learning? What evidence do you have to back up that assertion?

What feedback do I provide the students? What do they do with that feedback?

Have I used a range of instructional strategies?

Which students are engaged in the lesson? Which are not? Why?

How do I communicate high expectations to learners?

What is the nature of the questions (surface, deep, or transfer)?

Is the classroom managed effectively? What evidence do I have to back my assertion?

Other Comments

Closing Moves (5 minutes)

- Ask participants to rate how well the team executed the protocol and followed agreements.

Copyright © 2019 by Corwin. All rights reserved. Reprinted from *Developing Expert Learners: A Roadmap for Growing Confident and Competent Students* by Michael McDowell. Thousand Oaks, CA: Corwin, www.corwin.com. Reproduction authorized for educational use by educators, local school sites, and/or noncommercial or nonprofit entities that have purchased the book.

Collective Efficacy: Developing Efficacy and Expertise as Professionals

Resource 6.12

Tools for Measuring Efficacy and Expertise

Resource 6.12a

Effect Size Tool

The data in Figure 6.12a show progress and proficiency for 30 students. The table includes an effect size for the class as well as the individual effect size for each learner. One way to develop this data on your own is to download the Progress vs. Achievement tool from http://visiblelearningplus.com/resources.

Figure 6.12a **Effect Size Data From a Middle School Forestry Class**

Name	Time 1 (Pre)	Time 2 (Post)	Individual Effect Size
Student 29	52	58	0.47
Student 14	33	60	2.09
Student 23	55	61	0.47
Student 11	44	63	1.47
Student 6	41	64	1.78
Student 26	61	64	0.23
Student 20	54	64	0.78
Student 22	63	65	0.16
Student 2	58	67	0.70
Student 12	53	70	1.32
Student 5	62	71	0.70
Student 30	68	71	0.23
Student 13	61	71	0.78

Key

< .0
0.01–0.399
0.4–0.799
≥ .8

Name	Time 1 (Pre)	Time 2 (Post)	Individual Effect Size
Student 7	70	72	0.16
Student 1	64	72	0.62
Student 18	71	73	0.16
Student 24	71	74	0.23
Student 17	54	74	1.55
Student 3	72	75	0.23
Student 21	75	75	0.00
Student 19	71	77	0.47
Student 27	74	81	0.54
Student 10	75	85	0.78
Student 8	83	86	0.23
Student 25	83	86	0.23
Student 15	85	96	0.85
Student 16	90	90	0.00
Student 4	84	91	0.54
Student 9	91	92	0.08
Student 28	89	94	0.39

Average	66.90	74.73	
Standard deviation	14.90	10.88	
Average of spread		12.89	
Effect size		0.61	

Created using the Progress v. Achievement tool from http://visiblelearningplus.com/resources

Copyright © 2019 by Corwin. All rights reserved. Reprinted from *Developing Expert Learners: A Roadmap for Growing Confident and Competent Students* by Michael McDowell. Thousand Oaks, CA: Corwin, www.corwin.com. Reproduction authorized for educational use by educators, local school sites, and/or noncommercial or nonprofit entities that have purchased the book.

Resource 6.12b

Knowledge Gain Tool

The data in this table show the progress and proficiency for 27 students using a 4-point scale. The data include a knowledge gain score for the class as well as for each individual learner.

Knowledge Gain Model From a High School Technology Class

	Pre	Post	Knowledge Differential
Student 1	2	2.5	0.5
Student 2	1	3	2
Student 3	1.5	1.5	0
Student 4	2.5	3	0.5
Student 5	3	3	0
Student 6	3.5	4	0.5
Student 7	3.5	4	0.5
Student 8	4	4	0
Student 9	2	2.5	0.5
Student 10	1.5	2	0.5
Student 11	1.5	2	0.5
Student 12	2.5	2.5	0
Student 13	3	3	0
Student 14	2.5	2.5	0
Student 15	2	2	0
Student 16	1	1.5	0.5
Student 17	1.5	1.5	0
Student 18	2	2.5	0.5

	Pre	Post	Knowledge Differential
Student 19	2	2.5	0.5
Student 20	1.5	2	0.5
Student 21	1.5	2	0.5
Student 22	3	3	0
Student 23	3	3.5	0.5
Student 24	2	2.5	0.5
Student 25	1.5	2	0.5
Student 26	2	3	1
Student 27	2	2.5	0.5
Average	2.18518519	2.59259259	0.407407407

Copyright © 2019 by Corwin. All rights reserved. Reprinted from *Developing Expert Learners: A Roadmap for Growing Confident and Competent Students* by Michael McDowell. Thousand Oaks, CA: Corwin, www.corwin.com. Reproduction authorized for educational use by educators, local school sites, and/or noncommercial or nonprofit entities that have purchased the book.

Resource 6.12c

Survey Tool Example

This survey provides teachers with a means to capture students' opinions related to efficacy.

O: I know where I'm going in my learning, my current progress, and what next steps I need to take to get better. 1   2   3   4   5
O: I know what strategies I need to use at surface, deep, and transfer. 1   2   3   4   5
A: I seek ways to challenge myself in class. 1   2   3   4   5
A: I take action to improve upon mistakes I have made. 1   2   3   4   5
C: I actively seek feedback from others to improve. 1   2   3   4   5
C: I work with others to solve complex problems. 1   2   3   4   5

1 = This is not me. 2 = This is me when prompted. 3 = This is me occasionally. 4 = This represents me most of the time. 5 = This is me all the time.

Copyright © 2019 by Corwin. All rights reserved. Reprinted from *Developing Expert Learners: A Roadmap for Growing Confident and Competent Students* by Michael McDowell. Thousand Oaks, CA: Corwin, www.corwin.com. Reproduction authorized for educational use by educators, local school sites, and/or noncommercial or nonprofit entities that have purchased the book.

Resource 6.12d

Focus Group Activity

In the following activity, a teacher/leader selects five to seven students to form a focus group to engage in a discussion related to the three areas of efficacy (i.e., orientation, activation, and collaboration).

Step 1: Use the questions from Figure 6.12d (see Figure 0.8 for additional questions) to begin the group discussion and to prompt student thinking about their own learning.

Step 2: Share the responses (data) with other faculty and discuss.

Step 3: Determine next steps as a faculty team.

Consider filming the focus group discussion so that you can use the footage in a faculty meeting. Use Resource 6.2 the What? So What? Now What? Protocol to discuss the data from the video.

Figure 6.12d   Focus Group Sample Questions

Orientation	• Where are you going in your learning right now?
	• What is your goal?
	• Where are you now in your learning? How do you know your performance level?
	• What next step do you need to take to improve your learning?
	• How do you improve your learning? How do you know if you are improving?
Activation	• What does a good learner look like in your class?
	• What happens if you make a mistake in your class?
	• Are you a good learner? Why or why not?
	• If you're not a good learner, can you become one?

(Continued)

(Continued)

Collaboration	• How do you prefer to learn—on your own or with your peers? • Do you help others with their learning? How? • How do you know that the feedback you are giving is accurate? • How do you know the feedback you are receiving is accurate? • How do you feel about feedback?

Copyright © 2019 by Corwin. All rights reserved. Reprinted from *Developing Expert Learners: A Roadmap for Growing Confident and Competent Students* by Michael McDowell. Thousand Oaks, CA: Corwin, www.corwin.com. Reproduction authorized for educational use by educators, local school sites, and/or noncommercial or nonprofit entities that have purchased the book.

Resource 6.12e

Interview Activity

In this activity, a teacher interviews an individual student on the three areas of efficacy (i.e., orientation, activation, and collaboration) with the goal of using prompts to encourage the student to delve deeper into the understanding (and articulation) of their own learning.

Step 1: Begin the interview with the questions from Figure 6.12d (see Figure 0.8 for additional questions).

Step 2: Use prompts to encourage the student's deeper thinking:

- Would you mind giving me a few specific examples?
- Explain what assumptions may be operating when you say that.
- Tell me more.
- Did you always think this? If not, what changed?

Step 3: Share the responses (data) with other faculty and discuss.

Step 4: Determine next steps as a faculty team.

Consider filming the teacher/student interview so that you can use the footage in the faculty meeting. Use Resource 6.2 the What? So What? Now What? Protocol to discuss the data from the video.

Copyright © 2019 by Corwin. All rights reserved. Reprinted from *Developing Expert Learners: A Roadmap for Growing Confident and Competent Students* by Michael McDowell. Thousand Oaks, CA: Corwin, www.corwin.com. Reproduction authorized for educational use by educators, local school sites, and/or noncommercial or nonprofit entities that have purchased the book.

Resource 6.13

Examples of Data Collection and Analysis Tools

In the following example, a teacher is going to review their efficacy and expertise-based data with their colleagues and determine next steps to improve student learning. The teacher begins this process by having her learners take a short, six-question survey (Resource 6.12c) in October and again in February. The results of the survey can be seen in Figure 6.13a.

Figure 6.13a   Efficacy Progression Chart

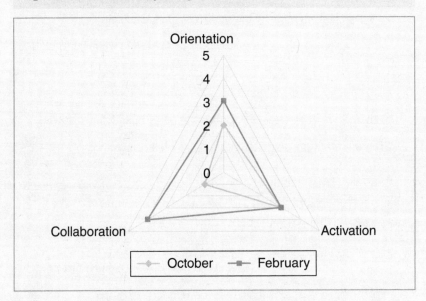

The teacher had students take a pre-assessment of academic content (in January) and then again about two thirds of the way through the unit (approximately seven weeks later) in February. She used effect size data to calculate growth and surface, deep, and transfer levels to denote progress (see Figure 6.12a for an example). In addition, she assessed students through classroom discussions (see Figure 6.13d Depth of Complexity Discussion Scaffold) and prepared data for her colleagues (see Figure 6.13e Depth of Complexity Discussion Data Collection Table).

The teacher then met with her colleagues and provided the following questions for the team to review:

- What do you notice about students' progress and proficiency in developing efficacy?

- What do you notice about students' progress and proficiency in developing expertise?

- What recommendations do you have for me to consider regarding improving students' progress and proficiency in developing efficacy and expertise?

The teacher's colleagues used Figure 6.13b Progress and Proficiency Matrix to categorize learner's progress and proficiency and used the team's Best Fit Impact Model to make recommendations to the teacher. Figure 6.13c Learning and Teacher Progress and Proficiency Structured Questions provides a way to engage students in the conversation about their learning with the teacher. The teachers' also recommended focusing on the element of activation, as it showed no growth for learners across the time periods assessed.

Figure 6.13b   Progress and Proficiency Matrix

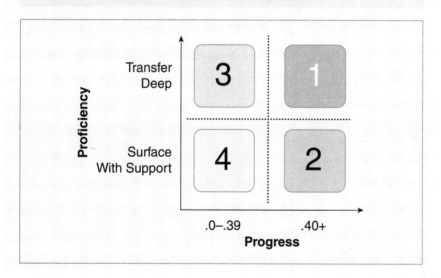

(Continued)

(Continued)

Figure 6.13c	Learning and Teacher Progress and Proficiency Structured Questions

	Learner	Teacher
1	• What strategies are moving learning forward from deep to transfer? • What will build efficacy (orientation, activation, and collaboration)? • What next steps will we take to progress?	• What strategies are moving learning forward? • What next steps will you take to ensure this student progresses in learning • How are you building student efficacy? What are your next steps?
2	• What strategies will move learning forward from surface to deep? • What will build efficacy (orientation, activation, and collaboration)? • What next steps will we take to progress?	• What strategies are moving learning forward? • What next steps will you take to ensure this student moves from surface to deep/ transfer? • How are you building student efficacy? What are your next steps?
3	• What actions are preventing deep to transfer learning?	• What are different ways for your strategies to move learning forward? Are there other strategies that may be better aligned to this student's learning needs?

	Learner	Teacher
	• What next steps will we take to ensure progress?	• What next steps will you take to ensure this student moves from deep to transfer? What next steps will you take to substantially move student learning forward?
		• How are you building student efficacy when they are stuck in their learning? What are your next steps?
4	• What actions are preventing you from moving from surface to deep learning?	• What are different ways for your strategies to move learning forward? Are there other strategies that may be better aligned to this student's learning needs?
	• How are we building and maintaining efficacy while we are stuck in our learning?	• What next steps will you take to ensure this student moves from surface to deep? What next steps will you take to substantially move student learning forward?
	• What next steps will we take to ensure our progress?	• How are you building student efficacy when they are stuck in their learning? What are your next steps?

(Continued)

(Continued)

Figure 6.13d	Depth of Complexity Discussion Scaffold	
Surface	**Deep**	**Transfer**
Questions	Questions	Questions
• Is this true? False? • How will you convince others this is true?	• How do you continue the pattern? What if ___ changed? • What reasonable estimations can we make here? • How does this relate to that? • Is this always true, sometimes true, or never true?	• What appear to be unique contextual considerations in the problem(s) you are facing? • How does context impact the core knowledge and skills that we are learning? • What are strengths and challenges of your solution and how do those differ from others?
• (S) What do you think are the most important facts and skills at play here?	• (D) What appears to be the relationship of x to y? • (D) What are other ways to think about or solve this problem? • (D) What appear to be the key relationships at play in the problem(s) you are facing?	• (T) How might this apply to ___? • (T) How do this connect to the situation in ___? • (T) How do this knowledge and these strategies enhance our ability to find a solution? • (T) What if x was changed? How would that impact your thinking and your solution? • (T) What appear to be the reasons why such challenges and problems persist?

Surface	Deep	Transfer
		• How might this knowledge and these skills play in other situations?
How will this knowledge support your learning?	What criteria appear to be important now in your learning?	What do you know now that you didn't know then (yesterday or at the beginning of unit)?

(Continued)

(Continued)

Figure 6.13e   Depth of Complexity Discussion Data Collection Table

	# of students that addressed question(s) initially (no additional prompting or after listening to other students)			# of students that addressed the question(s) after receiving prompts from the teacher or when listening to others			# of students that were unable to address the question(s) after receiving prompts from the teacher or when listening to others		
Surface-Level Questions	T1: 9	T2: 12	T3: 21	T1: 13	T2: 10	T3: 5	T1: 6	T2: 6	T3: 2
Deep-Level Questions	T1: 0	T2: 8	T3: 8	T1: 4	T2: 12	T3: 15	T1: 24	T2: 8	T3: 5
Transfer-Level Questions	T1: 0	T2: 2	T3: 8	T1: 4	T2: 6	T3: 8	T1: 24	T2: 20	T3: 12

Copyright © 2019 by Corwin. All rights reserved. Reprinted from *Developing Expert Learners: A Roadmap for Growing Confident and Competent Students* by Michael McDowell. Thousand Oaks, CA: Corwin, www.corwin.com. Reproduction authorized for educational use by educators, local school sites, and/or noncommercial or nonprofit entities that have purchased the book.

REFERENCES

Albion, P., & Gibson, I. (2000). Problem-based learning as a multimedia design framework in teacher education. *Journal of Technology and Teacher Education, 8,* 315–326.

Almarode, J., & Miller, A. M. (2017). *From snorkelers to scuba divers in the elementary science classroom: Strategies and lessons that move students towards deeper learning.* Thousand Oaks, CA: Corwin.

Bandura, A. (1993). Perceived self-efficacy in cognitive development and functioning. *Educational Psychologist, 28,* 117–148.

Bandura, A. (1997). *Self-efficacy: The exercise of control.* New York, NY: Freeman.

Bereiter, C. (2002). *Education and mind in the knowledge age.* Mahwah, NJ: Erlbaum.

Bjork, R. A. (1994). Memory and metamemory considerations in the training of human beings. In J. Metcalfe & A. Shimamura (Eds.), *Metacognition: Knowing about knowing* (pp. 185–205). Cambridge, MA: MIT Press.

Boser, U. (2018). Learning is a learned behavior. Here's how to get better at it. *Harvard Business Review.* Retrieved from https://hbr.org/2018/05/learning-is-a-learned-behavior-heres-how-to-get-better-at-it

Briceño, E. (2015, November 15). Growth mindset: Clearing up some common confusions. *KQED Mindshift.* Retrieved from http://ww2.kqed.org/mindshift/2015/11/16/growth-mindset-clearing-up-some-common-confusions/

Brookfield, S. (1989). *The power of critical theory for adult learning and teaching.* New York, NY: Open University Press.

Buck, S. (2018). *Green, yellow, and red cup signals.* Ross, CA: Ross School District.

Chamorro-Premuzic, T. (2015, March 25). Why group brainstorming is a waste of time. *Harvard Business Review.* Retrieved from https://hbr.org/2015/03/why-group-brainstorming-is-a-waste-of-time

Christensen, C. M., & Shu, K. (2006). *What is an organization's culture?* (Rev.; Harvard Business School Background Note 399-104). Cambridge, MA: Harvard Business School.

Clarke, S. (2014). *Outstanding formative assessment: Culture and practice.* Hachette, England: Hodder Education.

DeWitt, P. M. (2017). *Collaborative leadership: Six influences that matter most.* Thousand Oaks, CA: Corwin.

Doyle, W. (1986). Classroom organization and management. In M. C. Wittrock (Ed.), *Handbook of research on teaching* (3rd ed.). New York, NY: Macmillan.

DuFour, R., DuFour, R., Eaker, R., Many, T. W., & Mattos, M. (2016). *Learning by doing: A handbook for professional learning communities at work* (3rd ed.). Bloomington, IN: Solution Tree.

DuFour, R., & Marzano, R. (2011). *Leaders of learning: How district, school, and classroom leaders improve student achievement.* Bloomington, IN: Solution Tree.

Dumaine, B., (1994, September 5). The trouble with teams. *Fortune.*

Ericsson, A., & Pool, R. (2016). *Peak: Secrets from the new science of expertise.* New York, NY: Houghton Mifflin Harcourt.

facilitate. (n.d.). *Online Etymology Dictionary.* Retrieved from https://www.etymonline.com/search?q=facilitate

Fisher, D., Frey, N., & Hattie, J. (2016). *Visible learning for literacy, grades k–12: Implementing the practices that work best to accelerate student learning.* Thousand Oaks, CA: Corwin.

Fullan, M., & Quinn, J. (2018). *Coherence: The right drivers in action for schools, districts, and systems.* Thousand Oaks, CA: Corwin.

Gladwell, M. (2011). *Outliers: The story of success.* New York, NY: Back Bay Books.

Gladwell, M. (2013). *David and Goliath: Underdogs, misfits, and the art of battling giants.* New York, NY: Back Bay Books.

Hackman, J. R. (1987). The design of work teams. In J. Lorsch (Ed.), *Handbook of organizational behavior.* Englewood Cliffs, NJ: Prentice-Hall.

Hargreaves, A., Boyle, A., & Harris, A. (2014). *Uplifting leadership: How organizations, teams, and communities raise performance.* San Francisco, CA: Jossey-Bass.

Hattie, J. (2009). *Visible learning: A synthesis of over 800 meta-analyses relating to achievement.* New York, NY: Routledge.

Hattie, J. (2012). *Visible learning for teachers: Maximizing impact on learning.* Thousand Oaks, CA: Corwin.

Hattie, J. (2015). *What works best in education: The politics of collaborative expertise.* London, England: Pearson. Retrieved from: https://www.pearson.com/content/dam/corporate/global/pearson-dot-com/files/hattie/150526_ExpertiseWEB_V1.pdf

Hattie. J. (2018). *Collective teacher efficacy according to John Hattie.* Retrieved from https://visible-learning.org/2018/03/collective-teacher-efficacy-hattie/

Hattie, J., & Donoghue, G. (2016). Learning strategies: A synthesis and conceptual model. *npj Science of Learning.* https://www.nature.com/articles/npjscilearn201613

Hattie, J., & Timperley, H. (2007). The power of feedback. *Review of Educational Research, 77*(1), 81–112. Retrieved from http://education.qld.gov.au/staff/development/performance/resources/readings/power-feedback.pdf

Karp, H. (1980). Team building from a Gestalt perspective. In J. Pfeiffer & J. Jones (Eds.), *The 1980 annual handbook for group facilitators* (pp. 157–160). San Diego, CA: University Associates.

Katzenbach, J. R., & Smith, D. K. (1995). The discipline of teams. In A. A. Thompson Jr., A. J. Strickland III, & T. Robertson Kramer (Eds.), *Readings in strategic management* (5th ed., pp. 483–495). Chicago, IL: Irwin.

Lacy, S., Levin, J., & Pildes, E. (Producers), Lacy, S (Director). (2017). *Spielberg* [Motion Picture]. USA: HBO.

Levi, D., & Slem, C. (1995). Team work in research and development organizations: The characteristics of successful teams. *International Journal of Industrial Ergonomics, 16,* 29–42.

Lomas, J. D., Koedinger, K., Patel, N., Shodham, S, Poonwala, N., & Forlizzi, J. (2017). *Is difficulty overrated? The effects of choice, novelty and suspense on intrinsic motivation in educational games.* Paper presented at ACM CHI conference. doi: 10.1145/3025453.3025638

Marzano, R. J. (2009). *Formative assessment and standards-based grading: The classroom strategies series.* Bloomington, IN: Marzano Research Laboratory.

Marzano, R. J. (2010). *The highly engaged classroom.* Bloomington, IN: Marzano Research Laboratory.

Marzano, R. J. (2017). *The new art and science of teaching: More than fifty new instructional strategies for academic success.* Bloomington, IN: Solution Tree.

Marzano, R., & Waters, T. (2009). *District leadership that works: Striking the right balance.* Bloomington, IN: Solution Tree.

McDowell, M. (2009). *Group leadership in the PBL environment* (Doctoral dissertation). Retrieved from ProQuest. (3370197)

McDowell, M. (2017). *Rigorous PBL by Design: Three shifts for developing confident and competent learners.* Thousand Oaks, CA: Corwin.

McDowell, M. (2018). *The lead learner.* Thousand Oaks, CA: Corwin.

McLean Davies, L., Anderson, M., Deans, J., Dinham, S., Griffin, P., Kameniar, B., . . . & Tyler, D. (2013). Masterly preparation: Embedding clinical practice in a graduate pre-service teacher education programme. *Journal of Education for Teaching International Research and Pedagogy, 39*(1), 93–106.

McTighe, J. (2018). Three key questions on measuring learning. *Educational Leadership, 75*(5), 14–20.

Moyers, B. (Interviewer), & Ganz, M. (Interviewee). (2013). *Marshall Ganz on making social movements matter* [Interview transcript]. Retrieved from Billmoyers.com website: https://billmoyers.com/segment/marshall-ganz-on-making-social-movements-matter/

Muller, D. A. (2008). *Designing effective multimedia for physics education* (Doctoral dissertation). Retrieved from http://www.physics.usyd.edu.au/super/theses/PhD(Muller).pdf

National School Reform Faculty. (2018). Retrieved from https://www.nsrf harmony.org/protocols/

Nottingham, J. (2017a). *The learning challenge: How to guide your students through the learning pit to achieve deeper understanding.* Thousand Oaks, CA: Corwin Press.

Nottingham, J. (2017b). *The learning pit.* Retrieved from https://www.james nottingham.co.uk/learning-pit/

Nottingham, J. (2018). *Learning challenge lessons, elementary.* Thousand Oaks, CA: Corwin.

Nuthall, G. A. (2001). *The cultural myths and the realities of teaching and learning.* Unpublished Jean Herbison Lecture, 2001. Retrieved from http://www.educationalleaders.govt.nz/Pedagogy-and-assessment/Evidence-based-leadership/Data-gathering-and-analysis/The-cultural-myths-and-realities-of-teaching-and- learning

Nuthall, G. A. (2005, May). The cultural myths and the realities of teaching and learning: A personal journey. *Teachers College Record*, *107*(5), 895–934.

Nuthall, G. A. (2007). *The hidden lives of learners.* Wellington, New Zealand: New Zealand Council for Educational Research.

O'Brien, M. (1994). *Who's got the ball (and other nagging questions about team life): A player's guide for work teams.* San Francisco, CA: Jossey-Bass.

Ochoa, T. A., & Robinson, J. M. (2005). Revisiting group consensus: Collaborative learning dynamics during a problem-solving learning activity in education. *Teacher Education and Special Education*, *28*(1), 10–20. Retrieved from http://files.eric.ed.gov/fulltext/EJ696157.pdf

Ochoa, T. A., Gerber, M. M., Leafstedt, J. M., Hough, S., Kyle, S., Rogers-Adkinson, D., & Kumar, P. (2001). Web technology as a teaching tool: A multicultural special education case. *Educational Technology & Society*, *4*(1), 50–60.

Ochoa, T. A., Kelly, M. L., Stuart, S., & Rogers Adkinson, D. (in press). The impact of PBL technology on the preparation of teachers of English language learners. *Journal of Special Education Technology*, *19*(3).

Organisation for Economic Co-operation and Development. (2018). *Preparing our youth for an inclusive and sustainable world.* The OECD PISA global competence framework. Retrieved from https://www.oecd.org/pisa/Handbook-PISA-2018-Global-Competence.pdf

Schwarz, R. (2013). *The skilled facilitator: A comprehensive resource for consultants, facilitator, managers, trainers, and coaches* (2nd ed.). San Francisco, CA: Jossey-Bass.

Senge, P. (1994). *The fifth discipline: The art and practice of the learning organization.* New York, NY: Doubleday.

Simonton, D. K., (2011). Creativity and discovery as blind variation: Campbell's (1960) BVSR model after the half-century mark. *Review of General Psychology*, *15*(2), 158–174.

Stonefields Schools. (2018). *Learning.* Retrieved from https://www.stonefields.school.nz/page/Learning/

Tuckman, B. W., & Jensen, M. A. C. (1977). Stages of small group development revisited, *Group and Organizational Studies*, *2*, 419–427.

Wiliam, D. (2011). *Embedded formative assessment: Practical strategies and tools for K–12 teachers.* Bloomington, IN: Solution Tree.

Willingham, D. (2010). *Why don't students like school?: A cognitive scientist answers questions about how the mind works and what it means for the classroom.* San Francisco, CA: Jossey-Bass.

Zbar, V. (2013). *Generating whole-school improvement: The stages of sustained success.* East Melbourne, Victoria, Australia: Centre for Strategic Education.

INDEX

A SAGE Publishing Company

Helping educators make the greatest impact

CORWIN HAS ONE MISSION: to enhance education through intentional professional learning.

We build long-term relationships with our authors, educators, clients, and associations who partner with us to develop and continuously improve the best evidence-based practices that establish and support lifelong learning.

Confident Teachers, Inspired Learners

MICHAEL MCDOWELL

Find out how to make three shifts essential to improving PBL's overall effect by helping students discover, deepen, and then apply their learning to a world beyond them.

MICHAEL MCDOWELL

Practical examples, activities, and reflective questions take you step by step through the work of the learning leader, ensuring growth in core academic content and 21st century skills.

JANE KRAUSS, SUZIE BOSS

Explore strategies for integrating project learning into all main subject areas, across disciplines, and with current technology and social media.

JULIE STERN, NATHALIE LAURIAULT, KRISTA FERRARO, JULIET MOHNKERN

Uncover conceptual relationships and transfer them to new situations with this must-have road map for implementing concept-based teaching.

To order your copies, visit corwin.com

No matter where you are in your professional journey, Corwin aims to ease the many demands teachers face on a daily basis with accessible strategies that benefit ALL learners. Through research-based, high-quality content, we offer practical guidance on a wide range of topics, including curriculum planning, learning frameworks, classroom design and management, and much more. Our books, videos, consulting, and online resources are developed by renowned educators and designed for easy implementation that will provide tangible results for you and your students.

JAMES NOTTINGHAM

Challenge makes learning more interesting. Learn how to promote challenge, dialogue, and a growth mindset for student success in *The Learning Challenge.*

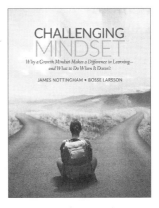

JAMES NOTTINGHAM, BOSSE LARSSON

Drawing on their work alongside Carol Dweck, the authors answer key questions about Dweck's theory of mindset and share proven strategies for mindset success.

JOHN ANTONETTI, TERRI STICE

Use the Powerful Task Rubric for Designing Student Work to analyze, design, and refine engaging tasks of learning.

GUY CLAXTON

Understand how "every lesson, every day" shapes the way students see themselves as learners.